BREAD & WAR

FELICITY SPECTOR

BREAD & WAR

A UKRAINIAN STORY OF FOOD, BRAVERY AND HOPE

DUCKWORTH

First published in the United Kingdom by Duckworth in 2025

Duckworth, an imprint of Duckworth Books Ltd.
1 Golden Court, Richmond, TW9 1EU, United Kingdom
www.duckworthbooks.co.uk

A catalogue record for this book is available from the British Library

Endpaper photos
Front left: Graffiti by TVBoy, Irpin.
Front top right: Meal in a summer kitchen at a village in Bessarabia.
Front bottom right: 'Poppyseed with roll' at Zavertailo cafe, Kyiv.
Back top left: Troops from a Marine battalion having lunch during a break from
frontline rotations. (Photo © Oleksandr Baron)
Back bottom left: The amazing table of food by Natalia at her volunteer canteen
near Pavlohrad, Dniepopetrovsk region.
Back right: Mural in Kyiv depicting a soldier with ears of wheat.

Typeset by PDQ Media

Printed and bound in Great Britain by CPI Group (UK) Ltd, Croydon CR0 4YY

The authorised representative in the EEA is Easy Access System Europe,
Mustamäe tee 50, 10621 Tallinn, Estonia.

Hardback ISBN: 9781914613784
eISBN: 9781914613791

For my parents, Cyril and Renee Spector
May their memories be a blessing

CONTENTS

BELARUS

POLAND

• LVIV

Carpathian Mtns

ROMANIA

MOLDOVA

Danube

1 IZMAIL
2 KRYNYCHNE
3 NOVI TROYAN
4 PLAKHTIIVKA
5 PALANCA
6 KOBLEVE
7 IRPIN
8 ANTONIVKA

9 POLTAVA
10 CHORNOBAIVKA
11 KAMYANKA
12 POKROVSK
13 DRUZHKIVKA
14 SLOVIANSK
15 LYMAN
16 SIVERSK

UKRAINE

RUSSIA

IV

KHARKIV •

⑩

IZYUM

⑨

⑪

EMENCHUK •

KRAMATORSK •

⑮

LUHANSK •

⑭

DNIPRO •

⑬

⑯

KOSTYANTINIVKA •

⑫

DONETSK

KOLAIV

ZAPORIZHZHYA

KHERSON

Nova Kakhovka
Dam

⑧

A

Crimea

ASTOPOL •

INTRODUCTION

This story begins and ends with bread, with its key ingredients of flour, water, time and hope; and the people who make small miracles happen, every day. Bread, because it is such an integral part of the Ukrainian table, in a country which grows wheat for half the world. It takes time and care and passion to make from scratch, and makes a meal complete. It brings some comfort to those who have lost everything, and those who are far from home. Despite bombing, electricity cuts, mobilisation and price rises, bakeries around Ukraine have managed to keep working. You can find the most delicious buckwheat loaves made in an oven powered by generators, pillowy soft buns filled with cherries and poppy seeds, or dough swirled around slow-cooked cabbage and salty *brinza* cheese. Their story during war is one of bravery, persistence and skill.

For almost two years I travelled back and forth to Ukraine, visiting bakeries helped by the organisation Bake for Ukraine, a small non-profit run by a group of friends from Odesa who had spent years working together in a restaurant supply business. They had a dual mission: promoting Ukrainian bread culture, while fundraising and sourcing equipment for small bakeries which made free bread for those most in need.

In Bucha, where Yaroslav had kept his hand-built bakery called Khatynka Pekarya going through the darkest times of occupation, and was still supplying his buns and loaves to the territorial defence and the National Guard. In Kharkiv, where a charity called Myrne Nebo had set up a soup kitchen and bakery, volunteers told me how they had crouched under metal tables during the worst bombing, coming back up again during pauses to continue making their bread. I spent weeks in Odesa where the energetic young chefs Illia and Viacheslav at DOU bakery were supplying hundreds of daily sourdough loaves to a local centre for refugees, and baked boxes of their special energy bars which they sent to friends fighting at the front.

I went along with volunteers as they delivered bread to front-line towns in the eastern Donetsk region near the border with occupied Luhansk, driving through silent ghostly streets lined with destroyed apartment blocks, where people lived in basements without water, electricity or light. In the small Kherson town of Chornobaivka, where repeated battles for a military airfield had turned it into a byword for Ukrainian resistance and Russian defeat, we unloaded boxes of bread in front of a boarded-up cultural centre, which had become a hub for aid. Our cars carried loaves through the country's highest risk red zone to the small town of Antonivka, where Russian forces with their deadly drones and snipers sat just two kilometres across the River Dnipro.

At a military hospital in the east, with a group of volunteer chefs who had gone to provide a day of fresh-cooked food and a boost to morale, I saw injured soldiers eagerly lining up for dark rye sandwiches filled with lard, and then lining up again for more. In a completely destroyed village in the east of Kharkiv region, I met farmers who had tried to pull mines from their land with their bare hands.

We stood together beside the burned-out wreckage of their homes, looking out over the fields where they had grown wheat and corn, where sunflowers had once reached towards the light, and talked of the day they would start farming it all again. I spoke to Tetiana, the young bakery owner in Kharkiv whose windows had been shattered by a rocket attack and heard how her customers had rallied round to clear up the mess and pay for repairs. My friend Katrya, a talented baker who had fled to Lviv from occupied Kherson, told me how she'd managed to pack her sourdough starter among the few precious possessions that she could carry, on a traumatic journey through the grey zone into free Ukraine.

I am left with a vivid memory of the first glimpse of the mobile bakery we had renovated and equipped, an old Swiss army vehicle which had ovens, a dough mixer and a generator already set up on board. We had tracked it down in the southern port of Izmail, and at the end of a long day testing it out, it had grown so late that the moon threw strange shadows on the walls, while we shared warm slices of sourdough dripping with melted butter. Someone shouted '*Slava Ukraini!*' – Glory to Ukraine. '*Heroyam slava!*' – Glory to heroes came the reply, and in that moment, it tasted like the best food in the world.

This is the story not just of that mobile bakery, but of the Ukrainians I met who farm and bake and open new businesses during a war, who champion local food culture, who volunteer and risk their lives to deliver supplies along the front. It is the story of unbearable loss, of courage, and a strong and proud Ukrainian heritage that refuses to die. And somehow, this story is always about bread.

February 2025

On a rooftop high above Kyiv, covered in camouflage, there is a disco lamp repurposed to light up the night sky, and a 1947 heavy machine gun mounted on a turret to shoot down Russian drones. It neatly sums up the mood in the city, three years after the full-scale invasion – ingenuity, resistance and determination. One of the men in this volunteer air defence unit is Oleksii, who I met while writing this book. He helps to run his family chocolate business by day, and spends nights or weekends with his fellow defenders on this rooftop, protecting the city from drones.

But there is a new and strange uncertainty about the future, after Trump's America started holding direct talks with Russia – and without Ukraine. People feel deeply disappointed, even betrayed, by the new, dark rhetoric coming from the USA. Although nights across Ukraine are still broken by alarms and the sound of explosions, in the morning people get up and buy coffee and go to work, soldiers continue fighting, volunteers still raise money and deliver supplies to those in need.

It is exhausting, after three years of war. But what you will not see here is surrender.

Part One

FLOUR & WATER

BAKING UNDER SIEGE

Chapter One
THE MOBILE BAKERY

If people cannot get to the bakery, then why not bring the bakery to them? One on wheels, which could travel anywhere, self-contained and self-efficient, resilient enough to cope with Ukraine's treacherous roads. The idea of a mobile bakery all began as a dream, a solution to food insecurity in front-line regions of Ukraine where infrastructure had been destroyed and people had been left with little access to fresh bread. Such a basic product, but one that was central to the history and culture of Ukraine, a country which grows wheat for half the world and where major holidays and festivals are so often marked by baking a special kind of ceremonial bread. A country where the terrible experience of the Stalin-made famine during the 1930s, the Holodomor, means people are brought up knowing that you never throw away a leftover loaf, not even a crust.

When the Russians launched their invasion in February 2022, life for Ukrainians was turned upside down. Around seven million women and children fled abroad, many braving shelling and air strikes on the dangerous roads west, while the borders were overwhelmed with huge crowds of humanity in search of safety. For those who stayed in Ukraine, living in wartime was suddenly filled with risk and uncertainty. Overnight, airports shut down and civilian air traffic was halted. Martial law was imposed, with a strict curfew in place – while businesses in Kyiv and across eastern and southern Ukraine hastily shuttered their doors. As a column of Russian tanks began advancing on the capital, days and nights were spent hiding in corridors or basements to the sound of bombing. It seemed utterly unconscionable that this could be happening in major cities in the very heart of Europe. Hundreds of thousands of Ukrainians rushed to defend their homes with weapons, lining up outside recruitment offices to join the armed forces or territorial defence, while others built barricades from sandbags, made crates of Molotov cocktails and learned how to fire guns. On the civilian side, people began coming up with innovative ways to help, with countless community-based initiatives to raise money for military units and provide practical support on the ground. Many food businesses turned their skills to feeding the millions of displaced people who'd lost their homes – some on their own initiative, others working with charities like World Central Kitchen. Restaurants and cafes which could no longer serve paying customers became temporary soup kitchens, while bakeries began baking bread to send to soldiers and people in need. It was a truly grassroots effort by people who were themselves living through absolute horror, yet had one thought – how to help those who were going through even worse.

That imperative was just as strong for many of the Ukrainians who found themselves trying to make a new life abroad. One of them was Maria Kalenska, who became the driving force behind many projects. She knew the answer to almost every question I asked and had a fierce and unyielding love for her family and her city, Odesa. She was the kind of woman who made things happen, with an encyclopaedic knowledge of Odesan food and culture. When the big war started she had been living with her family in Berlin. She had only just landed there, on the very last flight back from Odesa, before Ukraine's airspace abruptly slammed shut. Her first thought was how to help: she got together with some Ukrainian friends to collect aid and organise trucks, and then they began baking bread. They were proud to make real Ukrainian sourdough, using the starter that Maria had kept going for years. They could sell it to raise money and educate people about Ukraine's bread culture at the same time. If French baguettes were on restaurant menus all over the world, why not *palyanytsya*? And the place they found to bake in was itself unique, a mobile bakery used by a friend in Berlin which dated back more than fifty years. The Swiss army built a thousand or so of them back in the 1960s, one for each battalion. They were sturdy and built to last, with everything you need to bake hundreds of loaves of bread efficiently installed on board. There were three big deck ovens, powered by a wood-fired stove. There was a long cabinet down one side with shelves where baskets of dough could be left to prove, and a narrow table on the other side to cut and shape it. At the back was a large dough mixer and a diesel generator which could provide a constant electricity supply. Around a hundred of these vehicles had been donated by the Swiss to Ukraine a couple of decades ago, and Maria was certain that some of them must still be in good working order.

I first came across Bake for Ukraine online, after I had organised a convoy to take donated bakery equipment to Kyiv in the summer of 2022. I was not usually a person who organised convoys, but I had become involved with a separate fundraising initiative called Cook for Ukraine started by Olia Hercules and Alissa Timoshkina, and I found myself wanting to do even more. My grandparents had fled Ukraine more than a century before, from a city then called Yekaterinoslav, now Dnipro. I knew precisely nothing about their lives there, but I remember reading old books about life in the Jewish community, and imagining how they had lived and how they had left. In the 1980s, I had visited the old USSR numerous times, with the notoriously dreadful state tourist company called Intourist. In the early nineties, just as the Soviet Union was crashing apart, I became ITN's Moscow producer. It was a tumultuous time in news: we saw barricades in the streets of Moscow, statues of Communist leaders were toppled, and the bravery of people from Lithuania to Ukraine and Georgia helped those nations to forge their own independent future. Although the job was all-consuming, I came to detest living there, under those grey leaden skies with their overwhelming sense of fatalism. I thought of visiting Kyiv often, and Dnipro: 'I'll get there one day,' I thought, but it never quite worked out. My job in the newsroom took me all over Eastern Europe and then Washington, but somehow never Ukraine. When I finally got to Kyiv, in the summer of 2022, I could only wonder why I had not made more effort to get there decades before. In Bake for Ukraine, I found the friends and the sense of purpose I had been searching for. Over the next twelve months I returned as often as I could to spend time with the bakers they supported, and promised to do what I could to help turn the dream of a mobile bakery into a reality.

Then, after months of searching, a miracle happened. In summer 2023, one turned up for sale in the Danube port of Izmail, just a couple of hours' drive from Odesa. I put up a fundraising page, and thanks to the immense generosity of friends and strangers, I managed to collect all the money we needed for the mobile bakery, and travelled back to Odesa to meet up with the team. It was a beautiful summer morning when we drove to Izmail to buy the vehicle from a man called Vlad, who owned a small family bakery in the town. There were blue skies and only a slight breeze, the shores of the Danube lapping gently around the anti-tank hedgehogs which lined the shores. The car was packed with ingredients for the bread: bags of organic flour from Aleksyi, a local farmer, as well as milk and butter and bottled water. Maria had carefully tended to the precious sourdough starter the night before, tucking it into a plastic box where it bubbled and grew, straining against the lid in a vain bid to escape. In the car behind was Tatyana, a retired teacher and enthusiastic home baker who lived in a nearby village. She had volunteered to make the bread on board and was ready for a long day.

Rounding the corner into the yard, that first glimpse of the mobile bakery was a magical sight. A squat, solid trailer, painted dark grey, with a complicated-looking generator fixed into the back, and a man up a ladder on the roof installing a little chimney for the wood-fired stove. We clambered up the metal steps to look around, cranking open the oven doors to peer inside, switching everything on to see if it worked. There was water trickling out of the tap. The two-armed dough mixer looked ancient, but it juddered noisily into life, while a little fire was soon roaring away to power the ovens, the temperature gauge slowly ticking its way upwards.

Next step: actually baking some bread. Maria and Tatyana measured out the sourdough starter and slowly began adding flour and water to begin the dough. The act of baking bread became a communal effort: someone operated the mixer, someone weighed out ingredients, someone cut the dough and gently shaped it into soft, round loaves, ready to rest in their muslin-lined baskets. It was a narrow space inside the trailer and uncomfortably warm in the heat of the ovens, and it was necessary every so often to clamber back down the metal steps into the car park and get a few breaths of fresh air.

At lunchtime, while the dough was proving, Vlad led everyone around his commercial kitchen space next door, proudly showing off his range of bread and buns, and introducing his staff. He selected a couple of dark rye and raisin loaves from a rack, which he sliced up for lunch, served with some strong coffee in paper cups decorated with blue and yellow flowers and the slogan 'Be Optimistic'. There were some Soviet-era cakes: a pastry tart filled with a sweet swirl of marshmallow and jam, a multilayered chocolate creation sandwiched with cream, crumbly *rohalyky* biscuits stuffed with sweet apple. Back at the mobile bakery, a local television crew had turned up and managed to squeeze on board, ducking out of the way as Tatyana slashed the loaves with a razor and sprinkled flour through a stencil of the Ukrainian *tryzub* symbol, while Vlad manoeuvred the specially designed wooden paddle into the oven so that it could reach right to the back.

There was a quiet rhythm to the day: tip the dough out of its basket, slash into it, flour on top, push it into the oven, clean the table, start again with the next. It took around forty minutes for each batch of bread to bake properly, for sourdough has its own timetable and cannot be rushed. A proud moment, not just because the mobile bakery was finally fulfilling its purpose, being useful again, but because this was proper Ukrainian bread: an old heritage recipe from a family in southern Ukraine that went back generations. It was made from organic flour grown by a Ukrainian farmer, a product of that rich, black earth which fed half the world with its wheat. It was nutritious and natural and would keep beautifully fresh for days.

No one noticed that it was getting dark by the time the final loaves were pulled from the oven, their bronzed crusts slashed into a smile. But then a whole crowd of people assembled in the yard to celebrate: staff from the bakery, Vlad and his mother, plus the Bake for Ukraine team who had been on their feet for almost eleven hours. There was a cheer as the hot loaves were passed outside to join the rest, stacked on wire racks to cool down. Someone shouted '*Slava Ukraini!*', and as tradition demands everyone chorused back '*Heroyam slava!*', and it was a rare moment of spontaneous joy in those dark and difficult times. A trestle table was set up next to the truck, the yard lit only by moonlight and a couple of battery lamps, and someone from Vlad's bakery hurried out with a plate of cured lard and some butter. A few bottles of local wine and fruit juice appeared. Maria sliced into a loaf of bread, still hot from the oven, while Vlad's mother protested that it really wasn't good for you to eat bread while it was that warm. We decided to take the risk, and at that moment, eating slices of warm bread dripping in melted butter, it tasted better than any Michelin-starred meal. The rest of the bread was boxed up, to be donated to a local National Guard unit, who later sent back word that it had been very much enjoyed.

The task of getting the mobile bakery back to Odesa, where it could be repainted and then repaired, fell to Sasha, a strong and gentle man who was capable of solving any logistical problem. He managed to hire a long flatbed truck and a crane to hoist the ten-tonne contraption on board, and made plans with a workshop in the centre of Odesa where a volunteer art collective worked. They had been repainting cars for the military in camouflage patterns and had offered to paint the bakery in a fetching dark green with its bright-yellow slogan on the side: 'Bread is flour, water, salt, time and hope'. Nothing about this mission was straightforward: the city street was narrow and the small truck which had been commandeered to pull the bakery off the transporter and into the workshop was not powerful enough for the task. The mobile bakery lurched slightly and almost toppled onto its side, saved only by becoming wedged under a bus stop. Eventually a tractor was summoned: Ukrainian tractors had famously towed away captured Russian tanks, and they were perfectly capable of taking command of a ten-tonne bakery. A few tight three-point turns and it was somehow inside, where the young artists could apply their paint spray guns and redecoration skills to a fifty-year-old vehicle until it looked like new.

In the terrifying spring of 2022, when Russian forces had swept through a large area of southern territory, thousands of people had grabbed whatever they could carry and escaped to Ukrainian-held land. Many of them had ended up in Odesa, which was relatively safe compared to cities like Mykolaiv and Kriviy Rih, which were coming under intense bombardment. There was an aid hub in central Odesa which was happy to take as much bread as we could give them for displaced families who came there daily to collect everything they needed for the new life they had never wanted.

The mobile bakery soon found a semi-permanent home, inside a corner of Shevchenko Park called the Green Theatre. The space had been built as a concert venue in Soviet times, and had enjoyed a few recent years as an open-air theatre again, until the pandemic and then the full-scale war had closed it down. It was run by a local philanthropist and businessman, who had invited a new volunteer initiative to set up a summer camp, with activities for children and a space for NGOs and charities to hold workshops and mentoring events. It was the perfect spot for the bakery, tucked away under some trees with its own water and electricity supply, and Oleg, a company manager turned baking volunteer, took charge of running it. Ukrainian journalists came to film it, and a famous photographer from Los Angeles took photos of Oleg at work. It was the kind of life which became known as war–life balance. Getting up at dawn to volunteer for hours, before the regular job started, with no time left for vacation or a day off. Other bakers came to visit and see how this unique old bakery worked in practice: a friend called Yaroslav travelled down from his Khatynka Pekarya bakery in Bucha, while a sourdough maker called Alexandre came all the way from London. They wrote down geekish sourdough calculations like hydration ratios and temperatures. They tried out wholewheat loaves and researched some old recipes using rye, which was more nutritious and lasted longer, although given the choice, everyone always asked for white bread. One night, while the team was working particularly late, one of the park security guards turned up with a bag full of fruit, picked from his mother's garden. There were sweet, juicy plums and tart apples, and it was a simple act of kindness which everyone would remember for a long time.

One early autumn day, the Green Theatre organisers had laid on a small craft market, to raise money for various good causes, and Oleg baked dozens of loaves to sell for donations. It was a warm, sunny Saturday, but like most days in Odesa, it was also a day filled with air raid sirens and warnings of missiles. It seemed that every time the craft market tried to open for business, the air alarm would come on again and everything had to shut down. Eventually, late in the afternoon, the skies grew calm and the market managed to stay open; people came and bought bracelets and embroidered blouses and loaves of bread, and children danced to the live music on the little open-air stage.

That summer, and into the autumn, the bakery was hard at work most mornings. After Oleg had arrived to fire up the ovens and get the dough ready to prove, someone would come to collect the bags of bread which had been prepared the night before, to take to the humanitarian aid hub in town. If there were many families waiting in line, they would slice the loaves in half and pack them in smaller bags, to make sure that there would be enough to go round. I wanted to try and do a test run further afield, to take the bread to people in the front-line city of Kherson. It was just a couple of hours' drive along the coast from Odesa, but life there was incredibly tough. Residents were subjected to constant shelling and drone attacks from Russians who were dug into fortified positions on the opposite bank of the River Dnipro.

I arrived in a suburb of Mykolaiv just after dawn on a summer's day, laden down with fifty loaves of sourdough which Oleg had made the night before in the mobile bakery. I had been put in touch with a volunteer called Steven who had promised to help me deliver it onwards to Kherson, where he suggested it could go to a man who looked after orphans. There was just one small problem, he confessed. 'I don't have a car, and I can't drive. But don't worry, we will get everything to Kherson!' A few minutes later he darted back. 'The honey man will take us!' I was confused. 'Who is the honey man?' 'The man who delivers our honey, of course!' A battered old car pulled up. Vitaly the honey man, who appeared to have brought a friend along for the ride, jumped out enthusiastically. He stacked the bags of bread into the boot, and off we set for Kherson.

To enter the city you need to get past a military roadblock, where they check who you are and what your purpose is. 'Volunteers! Bread!' Steven said, offering his documents to the guards. They took one look inside the car and waved us through, and we drove into the half-empty city to find the orphanage man. Steven asked to make a stop, to check in with a family whose house had just been damaged in a rocket attack. As we arrived, I could see that the charred remains of their roof had been stacked on the pavement along with a piece of the rocket. Steven found a ladder somewhere and climbed up to measure it for a tarpaulin cover. With the sound of incoming explosions in the distance, I noticed that among the debris was a page from a textbook, burned at the edges. It showed a 1903 photograph of Lenin giving a speech. You could hardly find a more appropriate image of Russian history, literally destroying itself.

The orphanage man, Volodymyr, white haired and with a distinct twinkle in his eye, arrived with a minivan decorated with stickers from a charity, and we began loading in the bread, along with plastic tubs of Vitaly's honey. He typed something into the translation app on his phone and held it out to me, a broad smile on his face. 'Why are you here?' it said, which seemed a reasonable question. 'We have brought this really good sourdough bread; we make it in Odesa in our mobile bakery. It isn't quite mobile yet, but it soon will be, and then we will deliver bread every day to Kherson. This is kind of a trial run. To show it's possible.' He smiled again and thanked me for the donation.

Later I found out that Volodymyr had saved scores of children from being abducted by the Russians during the long months of occupation. The second time we visited him, he showed us around the youth centre he was fitting out. On one wall was a cardboard tree with little cut-out hearts hanging from the branches, each one decorated with a photo of a child who he had managed to keep safe. Giving him bread didn't seem nearly enough, but it was something. A few months later our mobile bakery finally set off on the road to Mykolaiv, and we were able to bake hundreds of loaves for villages in a liberated region which was under constant Russian bombardment. The attacks made daily life in Kherson so miserable that tens of thousands of people fled. But tens of thousands of people had also stayed, so baking *palyanytsya*, the traditional Ukrainian bread, made by hand and with flour from local wheat, seemed a good way to honour the country's culinary heritage as well as bringing immediate, practical help.

But a lot of work lay ahead to make the bakery fully mobile. Project manager Sasha managed to find a mechanic who was excited about the idea of working on a decades-old and unfamiliar vehicle, and towed it to the grounds of his workshop on the edge of town. They found an old instruction manual and had it translated into Ukrainian. A man from Zurich got in touch to explain that he had served in the Swiss military as a baker and offered to share his experience of operating a mobile bakery in the field. Next would come a bigger challenge: taking the bakery on the road to provide a more consistent supply of bread to Kherson.

Chapter Two

GOOD BREAD TO THE FRONT LINE

'You should understand that the Russians see us. They see our cars, they see us deliver bread, they see us get out and make photos. And you should also understand that they really want to kill us.' Vlad Malashchenko, the twenty-eight-year-old owner of the Good Bread from Good People bakery, is driving a van filled with boxes of freshly baked bread along the impossibly treacherous road towards Siversk, a town in Donetsk region around five miles from the Russian front line. It is a nightmarish journey: all temporary bridges and dusty roads cut right through fields, military vehicles churning up the ground under the constant boom of artillery somewhere not far in the distance. High overhead, impossible to see, there could well be Russian drones, watching as our little convoy bumps its way towards the devastated town. At the turning towards a narrow pontoon bridge, a young soldier stands alone, waving vehicles through one at a time, like a traffic warden dressed in full combat gear. Armoured personnel carriers rumble past, and a succession of olive drab pickup trucks, some with British licence plates, covered by hand-woven camouflage nets. This is the most extreme form of food delivery you could possibly get.

It was hardly the kind of work which Good Bread had ever imagined they would do, but Vladyslav Malashchenko was used to defying the odds. He first set up the inclusive social enterprise bakery when he was just twenty-one years old. His parents had always worked with mentally disabled children, and he says he realised there was next to no provision for adults. Although he had studied at theatre school and dreamed of becoming a film director, he had also trained as a remedial teacher and found that Ukraine treated people with mental disabilities like second-class citizens: there was no help for them to get proper job training, to get married and have children, to live a normal life. He had just 150,000 hryvnias – around £4,000, to put towards his bakery project – and somehow made it happen, gathering donations from friends and supporters on Patreon, to keep it going. He built a social enterprise which would not only give mentally disabled people a skill for life, but would begin changing attitudes across Ukrainian society – and help all people to be treated with dignity and respect.

Before the war, the bakery made cupcakes, croissants and tarts which were not only available commercially, but had a philanthropic twist: you could pay for an 'invisible cake' – which would then be given for free to someone else in need. There were plans to open a cafe. But as soon as the full-scale invasion began, the Good Bread team realised nobody would need cupcakes; as the citizens of Kyiv rallied to defend the capital from the advancing Russian forces, they reopened their doors and began baking simple loaves of bread for soldiers and civilian defenders. First of all Vlad put out a request for volunteers to come and help. Then their mentally disabled workers began coming back too, and soon Good Bread was turning out hundreds of loaves a day. By late 2023 they were able to move to a new hub on Kyiv's left bank, with around twenty-four staff members working alongside mentors and volunteers.

The aim has always been to recreate a nurturing atmosphere which treats employees like part of the family. Having the extra space in their new site has allowed them to expand their range beyond the more simple white loaves which they ship to the east: there is now sourdough, plaited challah bread and a small range of cakes, which they sell at a bimonthly market in central Kyiv. There is even an art therapy space upstairs – a big, bright room full of books and art materials, where people can come and draw or paint, and take part in master classes or workshops.

There is rarely any drama at Good Bread; rather, a distinct air of calm. Each day begins by turning on the huge spiral mixers, rhythmically kneading dough, while bakers in their neat grey uniforms with T-shirts declaring 'Not Broken', begin weighing out exact portions, shaping them efficiently into batons, placing them neatly into bread tins. They practise the kind of efficient, clockwork motion you will see in any professional bakery: in one corner, racks of tins are wheeled into a proving room, until they are ready to be ferried into the steam and heat of the deck ovens. Along a long table by the window there is a constant clatter as finished bread is tipped out and stacked onto racks, until it has cooled enough to be packed into large boxes ready for the long journey south or east. One wall displays a whiteboard with a list of place names and numbers: these are the destinations where the volunteers will be heading and the quantity of bread they will take. Over the months this list of names has become part of the ugly lexicon of Russia's war: Bakhmut, Avdiivka, Kupyansk, Chasiv Yar. Once a day a lorry or some smaller vans will park in the courtyard to be loaded up with boxes of bread. One volunteer says helping with the deliveries has been incredibly humbling: he talks of a lady who had been living in a tent for shelter, who pressed a jar of pickled vegetables into his hands as thanks. Another insists that it's important not to judge the people who choose to stay in such extreme and distressing surroundings: 'We need to remember that our job is just to bring bread.'

Two years into the war, they were continuing to bring bread to those in need, and I joined the volunteers on the day-and-a-half-long drive from Kyiv to Donetsk region in the east. The first destination was Kostyantinivka, where the road turns off towards Bakhmut, where Vlad had arranged to drop off bread at a volunteer space providing practical help for soldiers just back from the zero line, where direct combat takes place. Inside, the walls were unexpectedly decked out in shocking pink: in a former life, this had been a beauty parlour. There were shelves neatly stacked with hairdryers, soap and shampoo, and there were showers and a room with washing machines, so that soldiers who had spent days in the freezing mud could wash and get clean clothes. No one was fazed by the ultra-feminine decor; indeed, they seemed happy to see it, volunteers taking bags of filthy combat clothes off their hands, ready with towels and hot tea and a place that for a few brief moments at least was 'not war'. Two women crouched in the back of a battered old van by the entrance, sorting through a mountain of tightly wrapped loaves. Many of Kostyantinivka's residents came there for shelter after fleeing homes occupied or destroyed by the Russian army, but a few weeks into 2024, just a few miles from the increasingly fluid grey zone, the place was itself turning into a battleground. Some days earlier, a guided air bomb and four S-300 missiles had destroyed the railway station, slamming into shops and nearby homes right in the centre of town.

We bump across railway tracks and through a long alleyway flanked by huge, empty concrete buildings, towards a hangar which is being used as an aid warehouse. 'It looks like the set of a film,' Yuri the driver remarks, revving the engine while boxes are stashed on board to take north to Lyman, where there's another humanitarian hub waiting to receive supplies. It is the middle of a weekday morning but there is barely anyone outside. On the other side of the empty town square, the only decoration is an old hoarding which someone has painted with the slogan 'Lyman is Ukraine'. Behind it is a destroyed three-storey building which was once a school. The structure is completely wrecked, but inside it is still possible to make out a Snow White mural on one crumbling wall, while on another is the remains of a brightly coloured map of Ukraine with the words to the national anthem taped underneath. The school's roof is entirely gone; the staircase opens straight onto the sky. Tattered posters stuck to the doorway show information about how to arrange evacuation. But we are driving the other way, further east along the Luhansk road, to Siversk.

There are things you notice along these roads, apart from the incessant swerving around the jagged potholes. Pretty much every vehicle which passes is military. Vlad says that a few months ago there were far more volunteer cars, but now hardly anyone comes; people are understandably exhausted, depleted of funds and resources, leaving places like Siversk increasingly forgotten and alone: 'If we did not drive here, perhaps they would have nothing fresh to eat.' A few enterprises remain strung along the road, despite the dangerous location – tyre repair shops mingle with shawarma stands, catering for the twin essentials of life on the front line. We pass a small row of kebab stalls with military vehicles parked up outside, soldiers jumping down from a tank to grab something hot to eat, snatching a brief moment or two of almost-normality.

The air seems somehow different in Siversk, cold and hard, as if robbed of oxygen. The sounds of artillery are much louder: 'Out,' says Yuri, and counts to five before another bang. 'And in.' Pretty much every building is badly damaged: we drive past endless empty blocks of flats with gaping holes, burned-out windows, shattered roofs. Around ten thousand people once lived in Siversk; now there are just a few hundred residents left, those who simply refuse to leave, somehow surviving all this time in basements without electricity or water supplies, without internet or telephone lines, without any of the resources that make up modern life. Stray dogs and cats run around; there are huge bomb craters and great heaping skips of rubbish – it's hard to imagine anyone coming here to collect it.

A couple of men are waiting at the corner of a large courtyard where planks of wood and crates have been piled up in front of a doorway to protect a makeshift medical clinic. Vlad works out that eleven people are living in the basement underneath, while around forty others come there to get whatever medical help is on offer. Some boxes of bread are swiftly carried inside, and then we promptly move on to another basement, with a handwritten sign outside declaring 'People'. Inside, some seventy people are living below ground. A couple of elderly women are moving about, wearing battery-operated head lamps; one of them starts to fry grated carrots and onions on a small wood-fired stove. A man suddenly emerges, waving a trap containing a large rat – vermin are a major hazard, flourishing amid the piles of uncollected rubbish. The residents accept some supplies, and Vlad asks where other people are living so he can deliver more. We clamber down into yet another basement where residents are hiding; a man comes out to take the bread boxes, while his wife opens a thick curtain just a crack to peer out and say thanks. A dim light flickers – a candle, perhaps, or a battery lamp. There's a religious icon taped to the wall, and at least some shelter away from the biting cold. The woman backs away, closes the curtain, social interaction done.

Back outside, two local men climb into our van to give directions to more residents who need some of the bread: 'Be careful, it's a really bad road.' We stop by a row of houses, and a few people come running out, glad to see the delivery. It is so hard to comprehend why they stay, living in this utter horrorscape: some refuse to leave the place where their loved ones are buried, others simply insist it is their home and they have nowhere else to go. 'Today in Siversk, I spoke to some of the women about their life,' Vlad says, 'and every time they speak about this bread which we bring from Kyiv – they say we love you, we love your bread. It's a big risk for us to come here, but we understand it's one of our missions.' It is not a place you want to hang around for long; even standing together outside the vehicle could attract the wrong sort of attention. You have to watch where you walk in case of unexploded munitions, while volunteer cars on the very same road a few days earlier had been targeted by drones.

Vlad had wanted to take bread to an even more dangerous town, Chasiv Yar, near Bakhmut, but it had already become so risky that volunteers were no longer allowed to travel there at all. Instead, once we reach the relative civilisation of a proper asphalt road and the bright lights of a gas station, Vlad meets up with the town's mayor, who is still able to get access to Chasiv Yar, transferring all the leftover bread into the back of his van so he can take it there in the morning. He worries constantly about the dwindling number of aid workers, and declares that volunteers should be exempt from military mobilisation. 'For me, if I didn't have a bakery which makes thousands of loaves of bread every week, yes – I would go to the army. But being a volunteer is not military, and it is not civilian, it's kind of in the middle. And you should have some protection from the government: you make so much bread, you help so many people, so maybe you need to keep doing it.' Like his colleague Dima, who regularly drives to the front with lorryloads of food. 'Everyone knows him, every person loves him, every person knows who Dima is, this guy from Kharkiv who comes to help us and to make something for us.' If he was drafted into the army, who would come then?

One sunny day, on the cusp of autumn 2024, Good Bread throws a small party to celebrate their seventh birthday. They have baked a giant loaf of bread in the shape of the number seven, and there is cake. Vlad has started another fundraiser to turn the fourth floor of their building into a space for lecture rooms and movie screenings, along with some supported accommodation. He has launched another humanitarian project in a smaller kitchen area behind the main bakery: a team has begun making hot meals for elderly and displaced people which will be portioned into individual boxes and distributed around Kyiv by Caritas, a Catholic charity. Half a dozen Good Bread employees are busily spooning buckwheat and meatballs and beetroot salad into plastic boxes, sealing them in foil with neatly sliced packets of bread. Yuri, the driver from the Donetsk region trip, turns up with an estate car to deliver it all to the charity offices a couple of miles away. A queue of people are waiting patiently outside, while a Caritas volunteer checks their names on a list and hands over the meals they've been assigned. An elderly gentleman stoops towards his bag, carefully putting away the warm package; his hands shake a little as he accepts a bag of walnuts to take away too. Next in line is a younger woman, able to collect dinner for her whole family. At this early stage, Good Bread can supply around 150 meals, two days a week, but they have plans to scale it up, if funds allow.

Vlad Malashchenko makes it his business to embrace new challenges, from taking on society's treatment of mentally disabled people, to the first days of war, when he and his colleagues set about feeding the citizen soldiers who rushed to the defence of Kyiv, to personally delivering food to the front lines. 'I understand that I can't stop, because there are so many people who need help,' he says. 'I realise it is only bread, but in our Ukrainian mentality, people know that if you have bread on the table, you have food. So I can't stop.'

Chapter Three

ACTS OF FAITH

'Welcome to Kharkiv, Hero City', says the sign, looming above the highway as you drive into town. Nowadays it is also known as Iron City, with unbreakable reinforced concrete running through its soul. It sits in the north-east, just thirty miles from the Russian border, close enough to come under relentless attack from modified glide bombs, which fly so low that they are impossible to detect on radar, or shoot down. In the first year alone of the full-scale war, some six thousand buildings were destroyed: universities, supermarkets, kindergartens, publishing houses and countless homes. But Kharkiv is doing its best to keep thriving, as it has done for hundreds of years. There are memorials everywhere to the year it was founded, at the heart of a Cossack settlement in 1654. It was briefly the capital of Soviet Ukraine in the 1920s, and the focus of a horrific atrocity known as the Executed Renaissance, when a generation of Ukrainian writers were arrested and killed by Moscow's secret police. It is a meeting place of two rivers, and boasts Europe's largest city square, where the skyline is dominated by a vast constructivist skyscraper called Derzhprom, the House of State Industry. It has a tractor factory so large that an entire district is named after it. And it is also a city of religious diversity, where a sizeable Jewish community is flourishing once again.

Tens of thousands of Jews began returning to Kharkiv after the Second World War, but it was impossible to practise their religion in Stalin's USSR. The last remaining synagogue was closed down in 1949 and turned into a sports hall. A decade later, Jews were still being arrested for baking matzo, the unleavened bread eaten over Passover.

In the early nineties, after the Gorbachev government handed back the city's Choral Synagogue to the Jewish community, Moshe Moskovitz arrived from America to take charge as chief rabbi. More than thirty years later, he is still there, and the *shul* has transformed itself back into a key part of Kharkiv's community.

As Russian forces surged across the border in February 2022, the Moskovitzes managed to take in around 150 local people, offering them shelter inside the synagogue. They helped to organise evacuation convoys for those who wanted to get out of harm's way, and then left for Israel themselves. But it wasn't long before they decided that their mission was to be back among their people in Kharkiv. 'When we came back from Israel, a man asked us to come and put up a mezuzah on his factory which had been hit. He just wanted to know it was there, even when the plant wasn't working.' They had spent decades doing everything they could to build relations between the city and the Jewish community, and even during the blackout of 2022, they managed to organise a ceremony to light a menorah during Hanukkah. 'We asked if we could put it down in the metro. It's a safe place and also symbolic because thousands of people were living down there during the first months of the war. They said go for it, and the mayor of Kharkiv came to light it with us.'

Their humanitarian deliveries which they've been doing ever since have helped to consolidate that close relationship, the rabbi's wife Miriam said. 'On one of our trips we were taking bread to local people and a group of soldiers were walking nearby. They called out to us, saying hello, and then one of them said "Shalom!". We had around twenty loaves of fresh bread in the car and we gave it to them, and this soldier started crying. He said, "I've been at the front for months and this is the first time I have seen fresh bread." And I realised – wow, this really is something which makes you feel human, instead of living on crackers out of a packet or whatever, you can feel normal again.'

They had started doing a special delivery to some Jewish soldiers serving on the front near Kupyansk, in the north of Kharkiv region. 'It's only an hour and a half away, so quite often they'll go there and take a box of warm bread, it's definitely something that's important.' The couple have certainly lived through some seismic times. The day before the full-scale war they'd been celebrating the thirty-year anniversary of their synagogue school. 'Three hundred children were there, balloons, everything.' Education was rapidly moved online, although they have managed to let children come in for a few classes.

From the very start of the war, charities and religious groups threw themselves into the massive grassroots effort to help the country to survive. There was a kitchen in the synagogue basement, and it immediately began turning out food and bread for anyone who needed it. When I visited them almost two years later, they were still working. 'At the beginning of the war, our cook just stayed,' Miriam told me. 'She just moved into the space downstairs and never left. There was shelling all over the place, but everyone down here felt kind of safe, they just thought no one would bomb a synagogue.' Since the kitchen was busy working, they decided to take food to members of the community. 'I often drive myself,'

Rabbi Moshe said. 'We take a van a few times a week to some of the villages where there is really war. We go to hospitals, to soldiers, to Jewish people and those who aren't Jewish. We bake a few hundred loaves of bread and donate it through the whole city. Fresh bread is such a significant thing, it makes people feel that we haven't forgotten them.'

Their humanitarian work continued despite the relentless bombing, and the energy blackouts which became the hallmark of early 2024. 'People who have stayed living here the whole time, they've gone through really tough times. So everything we can do for them, every day we are here is very special. It's just better not to look at the news every day.' Not that it's easy to avoid the news, when it comes directly to your home in Kharkiv. The day before the October 7th Hamas attack in Israel, Iskender missiles landed right next to the Moskovitz family's house. 'The missile hit, all the windows flew out, we were at home at the time. I mean, this is life in Ukraine,' Miriam said. 'The windows of the synagogue were smashed, it's just around the corner from where we live. We started giving out bread to the emergency workers. My kids were helping.'

We followed Miriam downstairs to the basement kitchen where some women were busy braiding challah: it was a Friday, and they were getting ready for Shabbat. There were some children playing in one of the rooms, while a few people wandered up to the kitchen, taking plates of soup and beetroot salad and sitting down to eat. They encouraged me to help with the challah baking, and somewhat clumsily, with several people watching, I managed to cobble together a creditable four-strand loaf. Before we left, Miriam rushed downstairs and came back with a bag containing the slightly wonky bread, still warm from the oven. '*Shabbat shalom*,' she said, and offered me an open invitation to Friday-night dinner at her home.

From Kharkiv, I took a train a few hours south to Dnipro, the city my grandparents had left more than a century ago. They had passed away many years before I was born and I knew next to nothing about their life. What I thought I understood was why they had fled – the pogrom where 120 Jews lost their lives in 1905. There are now around 45,000 Jews in modern-day Dnipro, and I was excited to visit the heart of the community, the grand ten-storey Menorah centre. Two local friends joined me to translate, and the chief rabbi there, Shmuel Kamenetsky, took us up to the roof, the entire city spread out below, flinging out his hand to point out the view. 'You see that white building? And next to it is a small building, and next to that an even smaller one?' It was barely possible to make it out. 'When I arrived, that was the only synagogue. Now we have eight, not to mention this place.' Inside the centre, there was a hotel, two restaurants, a Holocaust Museum and even a hospital. All this in a city where Jewish life had been completely wiped out for decades. 'When we first arrived here, do you know how we reached out to the rest of the community? Food. We invited them to share our food.' The rabbi invited us to stay for breakfast, and at a kosher cafe on the ground floor, we ate plates of *syrniki* curd cheese pancakes and chopped salad with hummus and bread.

I had come to Dnipro in search of Jewish food, but especially to visit the matzo factory, Tiferet Hamatzot. During Soviet times, it was forbidden to make or eat matzo as part of the Communist crackdown on any outward display of Judaism. But for the last thirty years the factory had been baking handmade matzo under strict kosher supervision, becoming one of the most famous matzo suppliers in the world. It was a symbol of Jewish identity, free to flourish inside independent Ukraine. It continued to work after the full-scale invasion and in 2023 it was almost destroyed when a drone hit a neighbouring facility, causing a huge fire. It was right before Passover, their busiest time of the year, but fortunately firefighters managed to get the flames under control before they caused any serious damage to the bakery. Despite all the challenges, in 2024 they were still exporting their *shmurah*, or 'guarded' matzo, to dozens of countries, including the United States, Israel and parts of Africa. David, the *mashgiach* or supervisor, described the highly complicated process, starting with the wheat. 'We can't buy it on the market,' he explained. 'We go to the field when it isn't wet; there can't be any rain. A Jewish person has to harvest it; he should go with the combine driver and press the button to start it, so that the Jewish person is actually cutting the wheat.' It is then carefully stored, to keep dry, and then they mill around twelve tonnes a month into flour.

There were around eighty employees, all of them observant Jews, working six days a week with just the Sabbath off. Inside the factory, there was a completely separate room for the flour, the walls covered with drawings and Hebrew sayings, painted by a local illustrator. A woman was working inside, expertly weighing out portions into a jug and then waiting for a bell to ring, the signal for her to pass the flour through a hatch. On the other side, a man was waiting to start mixing it with water; from that moment, David would start the clock, counting down exactly eighteen minutes. That is designed to stop any sign of fermentation starting to take place, because Jewish law forbids any leavened bread during Passover. In the main part of the factory, with a digital display ticking down the minutes on the wall, the staff were hard at work. One man was bashing down the stiff flour-and-water dough mixture with a long metal pole into a more pliable texture, physically jumping up and down to put his full weight into it. On another table, some women were rolling out pieces of dough into thin rounds, then docking small holes with a metal plate to make doubly sure they didn't rise in the oven. David was patrolling around the whole time, occasionally checking the tabletops or peoples' hands, to make sure nothing was wet.

At the ovens, a couple of bakers were in charge, expertly flipping the matzo inside, where they took just a few seconds to bake. Little puffs of steam rose into the air as they were pulled out onto a rack, crisp and light and slightly charred around the edges. They were left to cool for a few moments before being stacked inside large wire baskets, ready to be packed in Tiferet Hamatzot's distinctive boxes. 'To carry on producing matzo for the rest of the world like this, it's kind of symbolic,' David said. 'The fact that in New York, you can buy matzo that is made in Ukraine, during a war, it really makes us proud.' The matzo are made of such simple ingredients but they are anything but basic: as you break off a piece you will rush to catch the crumbs, so as not to waste a single mouthful. The flavour sings of home and memory, mixed with the slightly acrid taste of fire.

That night, my Dnipro friends Yevhenii and Maya took me to a Jewish restaurant where I had one of the best hummus plates of my life, garlanded with fried potatoes and aubergine, chopped salad and a fudgy soft-boiled egg. The restaurant was called Moshe, which had been my grandfather's name, before he anglicised it to Maurice when they landed in London all those years ago. His name was one of the few things I knew about him, and I could not think of a more fitting end to the day. On the way home, we walked along the bank of the river, past the 'I Love Dnipro' sign, the water rippling gently under the moonlight. An air raid siren came on, and almost simultaneously the heavens opened with a downpour of torrential rain. The sudden claps of thunder sounded disconcertingly like air defence shooting down drones. In wartime Ukraine, you can never experience a thunderstorm in the same way again.

North Saltivka is a working-class area in northern Kharkiv whose rows of tower blocks had been pulverised by Russian shelling and artillery fire during the first months of the war. During that time, the Blahodat Baptist church, like the synagogue, had sheltered more than a hundred people in its basement for weeks on end. Pastor Dmytro and his volunteers got busy organising food, water and basic necessities, sleeping on chairs pushed together in the corridor. They established a soup kitchen in a portacabin outside the building, where people could come in the mornings to collect hot meals. Kharkiv did not fall, and instead, in the autumn of 2022, Ukrainian forces launched their successful counteroffensive, pushing the Russian occupiers out of Kharkiv region altogether. Towns like Izyum and Balaklia were liberated, the Ukrainian flag triumphantly flying above official buildings once again. Thousands of people who had left Kharkiv began slowly to return; for a while, the attacks on the city seemed less intense, and work began to fix up some of the buildings in Saltivka which were not destroyed beyond repair.

A year later, with the church still trying to supply aid and support for those who couldn't provide for themselves, Pastor Dmytro had begun thinking about setting up a bakery in a spare room in the basement, so that the church could begin delivering fresh bread. 'It came to me in a dream,' he said. 'And then I got a phone call from Maria at Bake for Ukraine, promising to help.' We walked around the devastated blocks of flats, while his church assistant Andrii told stories about how they'd ventured out to buy food and deliver it to elderly people during the worst of the shelling.

'We pulled up just over there,' he said, pointing to some traffic lights, 'because we saw someone we knew and stopped to talk to them. Moments later a shell landed, right where we would have been driving. We hid behind the car, although then I realised we were sheltering next to a gas station. If any shrapnel had flown there, there would have been nothing left.' Fortunately for them, nothing had landed near the petrol tanks.

The dream of the bakery finally became a reality after Bake for Ukraine managed to buy some cut-price equipment from a business in Odesa which was closing down, and had it all shipped straight to Kharkiv.

The week the church bakery began operating, I went back to see it in action. It was a cold winter day in early 2024 and the Russians had found a new way to torment Kharkiv, dropping 250-kilogram guided bombs on the city centre with depressing regularity. But down in that small basement room, there was quite the air of excitement, with six church volunteers crowded around a table, being shown what to do by Anna, who was a manager at the local bread factory. A large mixer was kneading some dough in one corner, while the volunteers were busy shaping different kinds of buns and batons, ferrying trays into the deck oven and taking finished loaves out to cool down. There was even a local television crew, trying in vain not to get in the way. 'All our volunteers have been helping out here since day one of the invasion,' Andrii said. 'They help to distribute medication and hygiene products, they prepare our hot meals. And they help with activities with children and displaced people.' Upstairs, portions of braised chicken and buckwheat were being handed out, along with some of the freshly baked rolls. Once the volunteers had taken the last trays out of the oven, they invited me to join them for lunch, where we tore into a couple of loaves of the warm, fluffy white bread. It was especially meaningful, they declared, to be involved in baking something as charged with religious significance as bread.

I had been told about another project involving the Baptist church: a Christian charity called Samaritan's Purse had been helping to install drinking water supplies in Mykolaiv, which had been without fresh tap water since the early weeks of the war. The Russians had bombed the main pipeline into the city, cutting off the supply altogether for more than a month. By the time it was restored, the network had been badly damaged and the non-potable water which rushed through it was much too salty to use. I met up with Pastor Viktor at his church in the north of the city, which had become one of the first sites for the charity's water pumps. It used the revolutionary reverse osmosis method to filter out toxic minerals without using added chemicals, apart from one bottle of cleaning solution which they had to run through the machine every couple of months. The church had been supplying clean water to residents for two years, through a row of taps fixed to the outside fence linked to a well deep underground. There was a constant queue of people there while we talked, filling up large plastic containers which they towed away in shopping trolleys or packed inside their cars. 'They can come any time from eight in the morning until six at night,' the pastor said, 'although if they are still waiting and it's after six we are not going to turn them away.'

The residents were grateful for the chance to get such good-quality water. I spoke to a scientist called Maria as she filled up an armful of plastic bottles with her day's supply. 'This is really excellent water, we are fortunate to have it here,' she said, adding that she had stayed in the city with her young family throughout the full-scale war. 'We rebuild our minds and our inside life to cope with this situation. We are all able to do it. As far as this water situation goes, older people usually manage to carry it away with them using a basket on wheels – although it's very difficult to get it upstairs. Especially when the electricity is off and there are no lifts, it is very hard.' Her resilience and courage in the face of such intolerable stress was astonishing; it was the kind of determination which I saw mirrored countless times in people I met across Ukraine.

Pastor Viktor was eager to show me the reverse osmosis machine, and I followed him down into the basement of the church. He explained proudly that it normally took many months of training for specialist engineers to look after this kind of equipment, but his volunteers had picked it up as they went along. 'When this charity offered to install it for us, I didn't believe it – we were the first to get it in the city centre. And when the heads of Samaritan's Purse came here and saw how we were managing to operate it, they decided to install all of their machines inside churches.' For a major city like Mykolaiv to lose access to fresh water has been incredibly difficult. 'Half a million people live here and it's impossible to live without water, it would be a catastrophe. Older people living on high floors find it especially hard. I saw how people were using water they took from rain pipes, it was a terrible time.' The best way forward was finding a sustainable way of coping, into the long term. 'At the beginning of this whole disaster, aid groups would bring in water on huge lorries, it would cost around $5,000 per lorry – so using water from underground is a much cheaper and more efficient option. And this water is for everyone, and for free.'

Back in Kharkiv's North Saltivka, the church volunteers had managed to keep up with their bread baking, although the relative calm of the last few months was proving short-lived. By late spring of 2024, Russia had begun massing thousands of troops at the border, relentlessly firing more guided bombs and missiles into Kharkiv and filling the skies with constant danger once again. After an especially horrible day of attacks on an Epicentre DIY store and other homes and small businesses in the city centre, I messaged Miriam Moskovitz over Telegram to see how everyone at the synagogue was doing. She sent me some photos of an event they had just held to mark the Jewish festival of Lag B'Omer. 'I thought no one would come because of what happened yesterday,' she said, 'but we had a beautiful celebration and hundreds of people turned up.' There were smiling children with balloons, people sitting around tables of food and men putting on *tefillin* to pray. It was a fleeting glimpse of a community determined to carry on with their most important traditions. Decades of political repression had not silenced their spirit, and neither would war.

Chapter Four

WE'RE HERE TO HELP

'I am here to fight for my city, not to die in it.' The last volunteer to leave the Kharkiv Hell's Kitchen that afternoon was calmly locking up, while everyone else hovered on the pavement outside, waiting for cabs. The team had been rushing to finish baking and pack everything away, after a very specific security alert warning everyone to leave the premises before four o'clock, when it seemed that a missile attack on the city centre was highly likely. The kitchen crew had reacted quickly, dividing dough into rolls, fitting as many trays as possible into the ovens, and ferrying the rest into the large walk-in fridge so it would keep without spoiling until the next day. There was no sense of panic; this was unfortunately just an average Tuesday afternoon, in a city under such relentless siege as Kharkiv.

The Hell's Kitchen charity was set up by Yehor and Lyuda Horoshko right at the start of the full-scale war. They were quiet, almost bookish, dressed for work in jeans and anoraks. They had left behind their jobs in IT to build the kitchen in a space underneath a fitness club in the centre of Kharkiv, providing around a thousand meals a day and 1,500 bread rolls, which they distributed to vulnerable communities across the region. From the outset, the couple decided to focus their work on hospitals, where they realised there was a great deal of need. 'They've been under a great deal of pressure. Many are closed, in front-line areas around Kupyansk and Vovchansk, while towns like Chuhuyev, to the east of here, are struggling with a heavy workload. As a result, a lot of people have to get treatment in Kharkiv. The hospitals there are very overcrowded, and they don't have budgets to feed people,' Lyuda said. 'So, we decided to concentrate on helping them, with both medical supplies and food.'

They managed to get financial support from some major international charities, including World Central Kitchen, set up by the American chef José Andrés, which had been doing incredible work on the ground supplying hot meals and essential food packs across Ukraine, as well as the UN's World Food Programme. A local church provided the flour. 'We work every day. Every Sunday we are here. We don't have weekends, or vacations. A few of us work seven days a week, although most of the volunteers are here three or even five days. Everyone works for free. But it isn't like normal work, because everyone has made a commitment to be here. Some since the very start of the war.' It is little wonder that most Ukrainians have seen a sharp fall in their household income. Most people have used up all their savings, while wages and small business earnings have plummeted too. It seems astonishing that so many are still willing to give so much of their time to volunteer for free. We were talking at the entrance to the basement kitchen, a maze of rooms festooned with patriotic flags, many of them signed by military brigades. The volunteers had come from all over the world: one was a former US Marine who had served in Vietnam. Another was a teenager from Ireland. Some of them had also been helping with the deliveries, driving bread and hot meals to villages close to the front.

For six months after the invasion, a huge area of Kharkiv region came under Russian occupation, including the town of Izyum, a key transport and logistics hub. It had been subjected to unimaginable horror. When it was liberated, in the autumn of 2022, Ukrainian troops found evidence of that horror in the forest on the outskirts of town, where hundreds of local people were buried in a mass grave. Some were killed during shelling, some when a missile had torn an entire block of flats in two. For others, the cause of death was simply unknown.

'We try to find the places where people really need help. For example, Izyum was in a bad situation after it was de-occupied,' Lyuda said. 'When all the volunteer groups heard about Izyum, they went there and unloaded big food trucks. But there are a lot of small villages where nobody has cars, and nobody can get to Izyum for these supplies. We take help to those places ourselves.'

They have tried to adapt the work of the kitchen to meet the city's ever-changing needs. In the months immediately after the invasion, many bread factories and shops had stopped working altogether. Two years later, the charity has made their operation more streamlined. 'We have teams, we have schedules, we know where to order and what supplies to buy, how to produce financial reports. When the war started many Ukrainians thought it would all stop in a few days. It was so hard to believe that your city would get bombed. It's impossible, nobody could be prepared.' The 'Hell's Kitchen' name is itself a reminder of the horrific conditions they lived under: 'For two months we were in a smaller space than we have now. People barely came outside. When big trucks arrived with supplies, we would rush out to unload them very fast, ten or fifteen minutes, because everyone was afraid for their families, their children. They were all living and sleeping for months down in the basement. So, we really felt that it was hell.'

The four o'clock deadline approached, when the security source had warned there would be bombing. The bags of bread rolls had been packaged up and handed over for delivery, the floors and surfaces had all been cleaned. As we stood on the pavement waiting for the cabs to arrive, I remember looking at my watch. It was about 4.15 p.m. but no one seemed the slightest bit agitated. An hour later, when everyone was safely at a cafe a couple of miles uptown, two guided bombs fell on the city centre, damaging at least six high-rise buildings and an animal shelter. We were too far from the scene to hear anything, just the angry sound of the missile alert app updating news of the attacks over and over again, the constant bearer of bad news. The kitchen team regularly posts its updates on social media during times like this: 'We are still working, despite the explosions outside!'

There are bakeries across Ukraine which have turned themselves into an essential part of the humanitarian aid effort, baking hundreds of thousands of free loaves which get delivered to people in need. When the full-scale invasion happened, and commercial businesses abruptly shut down, they filled a crucial gap, continuing to bake under curfew and sometimes under shelling, to make sure their local communities did not go without. I travelled to Izyum to meet volunteers from the Myrne Nebo charity, who showed me the deep basement underneath their kitchen space where they had lived during the fighting: it was dark and damp and cold even in the fierce heat of summer outside. It must have been freezing down there during the winter. After liberation, they were finally able to use it to store sacks of vegetables again. For a while they were the only bakery in the area, the only source of fresh bread for thousands of people. At their larger kitchen and baking space in Kharkiv, they were worried about how they would keep going after the end of a large grant which had paid for essential supplies and maintenance.

Small bakeries tried their best to continue donations while trying to restart their business activities again, once things began reopening. At DOU in Odesa, bakers Illia and Viacheslav had started supplying their sourdough loaves to a local refugee hub and their friends in the armed forces. Tens of thousands of people who fled the temporarily occupied regions further down the Black Sea coast like Mariupol and Kherson came to the relative safety of Odesa. DOU had barely been open for a couple of months when the invasion shattered normal life for ever. Illia and Viacheslav had wanted to start their own business baking sourdough for the city's restaurants. Their bakery was tucked away in a narrow space in the front of a grocery store in the centre of town, oven at the back, a long bench to shape the dough, cooling racks carefully slotted in the only available gap. They turned out beautiful, crusty loaves, burnished deep bronze; you could taste the rich flavour of the wheat and the slightly acidic tang of the sourdough starter. Sometimes they got hold of different flours and made seeded wholewheat, dark rye and buckwheat.

Gradually Odesa began opening back up again, the anti-tank hedgehogs receded from the city centre, the sandbags in front of Primorsky Boulevard were taken down, and the city's irrepressible spirit was given life again. Illia and Viacheslav were able to start supplying cafes, and they began baking cookies and granola which they could sell online or to customers who showed up at the door, banging on the window at the grocery shop entrance to get inside. The cookies were a hit: soft and chewy peanut butter filled with caramel, buckwheat with chocolate chips, dark chocolate with hazelnuts. Bake for Ukraine helped with donations, and every day they would pack loaves into bags for the refugee hub up the road, while a van would come to take more supplies to nearby villages.

Then in the winter of 2022 came a new catastrophe when Russia began systematically targeting civilian energy supplies, bombing thermal and hydroelectric power plants and electricity lines. When the city was plunged into darkness, without power for hours on end, it was impossible to bake bread. Sometimes there was enough electricity to switch the ovens on for a while, enough time to bake cookies, or the peanut butter energy bars they made for their friends at the front. Finally Bake for Ukraine helped them to find a generator and shipped it to Odesa, and then they could get up at four in the morning again, as they had always done, and walk through the dark streets of blackout at dawn, and fire up their ovens to make bread. The city was filled with generators that winter; there was no escape from the constant hum of the motors, or the smell of diesel in the air. But it kept the lights on, and medical clinics and schools and supermarkets and coffee shops could stay open, and DOU could continue baking bread. And when they raised money for the ingredients, they would bake trays of their special energy bars studded with prunes and raisins, and send them to the air defence and assault battalions defending the city.

Odesa came under fire most nights, drones snaking their way from occupied Crimea over the Black Sea. The sound of air defence shooting them down woke people up from their restless sleep, although some of them got so used to it they slept through wave after wave of attacks. In summer, when the muggy heat means you keep the windows open, it is impossible to escape the noise outside. You talk about nights being 'loud' as you drag the pillows and a blanket into the corridor, to move behind the relative safety of two walls. In the winter, behind thick curtains, sound alerts on the phone disabled, it is all too easy to choose sleep over caution. In the morning you finally see the long list of warnings which the missile app has been flinging out into the ether, and wonder how none of it managed to wake you up.

When Russia began destroying electricity plants again, Illia and Viacheslav dragged the generator back onto the pavement and tried their best to keep the ovens going, opening up at dawn and working seven days a week without fail. They eventually won a business grant to open a cafe, learned how to make good coffee and tried out recipes for sandwiches and brownies and breakfast food. In the mornings, a car would pull up beside the grocery shop and they would load up the boot with bags of just-baked bread for families who had left their homes far behind, and pensioners in high-rise flats who struggled to get outside when there was no power to work the lifts, and for the care home which looked after children with disabilities who giggled and laughed as they ran to collect their bread. It was heartbreaking, in this beautiful Black Sea city full of love and life, that there were so many people who were desperate for fresh bread.

The Khatynka Pekarya, or Baker's Hut, in Bucha, could hardly have looked more different. Yaroslav Burkivskiy had built it himself from clay and straw, in traditional Ukrainian style, after the restaurant where he had worked closed down during the pandemic. The building was nestled on the edge of the town, surrounded by plants and trees. Yurii, his fellow baker, had left a job in IT to become a baker. I was there with two friends – one who did the driving and another who came to take photos. War makes you glad to appreciate the basic things in life, he told us, as he patiently plaited sourdough buns filled with sweet soft cheese or apple jam. The bakery had been a lifeline for local people after the terrible weeks of Russian occupation. Miraculously, it had been left largely undamaged, and Yaroslav and his team managed somehow to get hold of scarce supplies of cooking oil and flour, giving away around 150 loaves a day to residents in desperate need of food. They slept on tables inside the bakery and worked in the dark, but they kept on baking bread, while those who could, left them donations of money or flour.

Bucha will for ever be synonymous with the horrific war crimes which the Russians committed there, and the searing images which emerged when it was liberated at the end of March 2022. But it also became a byword for resistance and survival, proof that even in the midst of such horror, all was not lost to darkness. Supporters from Poland helped to buy the bakery a large dough mixer, and they built a bigger wood-fired oven in the yard outside so that they could increase their capacity. As large foundations and charities helped to rebuild Bucha's shattered houses and burned-out blocks of flats, the Khatynka Pekarya no longer needed to give free bread away to residents. They managed to get business going again, baking a large range of sourdough bread and buns, which they displayed on a large table in the yard for customers to buy. Alongside that, thanks to continued donations from supporters, they were still able to bake free bread for the local National Guard.

The last time I visited, with a photographer friend, I watched Yurii at work all morning, calm and methodical with a rhythm which was almost mesmeric, transferring the bread into the outdoor oven, patting fresh dough into small pies stuffed with caramelised onion and cabbage and cheese. When the loaves were done he pulled them out on a wooden paddle, carefully brushing off the excess flour, and set them aside to cool down until the long trestle table was covered with golden baked goods, the glorious aroma of fresh bread and toasted seeds. 'There's no stability nowadays,' Yaroslav said. 'It's really hard to plan. Many people left the area, not everyone, but it is still a nervous time. The main thing is to maintain some kind of balance, to keep working and not to lose faith.' The bread was incredible, and we bought one of everything, standing in the car park to eat while the buns were still warm.

A few weeks later, Yurii was mobilised into the Ukrainian armed forces, and after his training he was deployed to the east. The bakery raised money to buy his unit a car and other equipment, bringing in well over their target from friends and supporters. Yaroslav drove the car filled with supplies to Donetsk region himself to hand it over, for this is what it means to run a small business in wartime Ukraine. Then, by the autumn of 2024, Yaroslav had also joined the armed forces, and the bakery was being looked after by his mother.

Chapter Five

THE MOBILE BAKERY ON THE ROAD

The road from Odesa to Kherson is lined with beauty and with loss. At first, it hugs the coastline on the edge of the Black Sea, winding through fields of sunflowers and wheat. You pass wind turbines and farmers riding tractors through their crops, and bus stops decorated with patterned mosaics. And then you look closer and see rows of the white concrete anti-tank pyramids called dragon's teeth, and bulldozers hewing great lines of trenches, stretching into the distance, dust billowing in their wake, and workmen in high-vis gear raking the black earth into mounds. You drive down the most beautiful stretch of road towards a town called Kobleve, which cuts through an estuary, so that the water glistens and ripples on both sides, and a signpost which looks like a heraldic symbol welcomes you to Mykolaiv. Soon you will see more notices warning of the danger of mines. On the other side of Mykolaiv, after the bridge over the Southern Bug river, you pick up the M14 highway. 'Kherson Region Welcomes You!' it says, only the first village you see is Posad Pokrovske, the skeletons of destroyed houses flanking the road, the remains of burned-out cars, the wreckage of a petrol station, and it seems that here there are only ruins.

It is a bright and sunny spring day, a couple of weeks before Easter in 2024, but there is not much traffic on this road. There are a few delivery lorries and the odd military vehicle in olive green. On the route into Kherson, there is a large building that looks like a gothic castle. Catching sight of the facade, disfigured by shrapnel marks and shattered windows, you imagine all the weddings and birthday parties which must once have filled the place with laughter and song. At the blockpost ahead of the city the soldiers open the back of the van to check the contents. 'Give me your phone, unlocked. Have you ever contacted anyone in Russia?' 'Of course not. Never.' 'What's in the van?' 'We are volunteers, delivering bread.' 'OK then, good, on you go.' You drive through suburbs with more empty streets, although there is always a woman on a bicycle, balancing bags of onions or tomatoes on the back, and a few pensioners waiting at the bomb shelter-slash-bus shelter for a ride into town. It is always surprising to see how many local bus services continue to run, but many people in these villages tend not to own personal cars and so it is the only way they can get around. On the north-west side of Kherson is the small town of Chornobaivka, which became the subject of countless memes at the start of the war after managing to fight off several attempts by Russian forces to storm its local airfield. This will be the first destination for the bread, after a journey which has taken many months to complete.

It hasn't been easy for volunteer groups to keep going for months on end. Many Ukrainian families live on less than $500 a month, according to a survey carried out in July 2024, while around 40 per cent of the population needs humanitarian assistance. Finding the resources as well as the energy to work for free on top of a full-time job and family commitments, not to mention the daily exhaustion of living under wartime conditions, has become a Herculean challenge. But the redoubtable Maria had managed to find a bright, cheerful office space for Bake for Ukraine in central Odesa, which a friend had offered to lend her for free. An entire wall was covered in coloured Post-it notes, setting out fundraising targets, logistics and tasks still to be done. The mobile bakery needed some comprehensive repairs: new wheels, a proper brake system, a rebuilt chassis. There were meetings with the local military authorities to get all the necessary permission. It had to be repainted in plain asphalt grey, the better to blend in with its surroundings. It took time to find the right wheels, and parts which the mechanic could work with. One night, during yet another Russian drone attack, one fell perilously close to the workshop where it was being repaired, setting off a fire. It was half past one in the morning, and Sasha rushed to the scene to make sure it wasn't damaged. 'Madame is safe,' he typed in the group chat, to everyone's relief.

There were detailed discussions with local Kherson contacts about security and where it would be safe enough for the mobile bakery to go. A village was chosen which seemed relatively quiet. Then a military friend who had been serving in the region came to the office to give his advice. He unrolled a large map on the table, jabbing his finger at various locations while he spoke. The quiet village, it turned out, had come under rocket attack that past weekend. He gestured at the map. 'You can't put it there. Definitely not there. I would not advise you to go here either.' In early 2024 the legal restrictions on access had become tougher, after three Western aid volunteers were killed in the town of Beryslav when their convoy came under Russian fire. Foreigners were no longer allowed into a large part of Kherson region, although Ukrainian volunteers could get in there as long as they had the right permission. But the situation was highly volatile. The military friend suggested that it would be far better to put the bakery in Mykolaiv, from where volunteers could then drive the relatively short distance into Kherson.

The Post-it notes multiplied on the office wall. Partners were found for a three-day trial run to check that everything worked. If you were an optimist, you might frame it this way: every problem is just a challenge waiting to be solved. Or maybe 'what can go wrong, will go wrong', but with the confidence that the mission would succeed, come what may, because Ukrainians can find a way to fix almost everything.

There was a beautiful plan which should have worked like clockwork. There would be a day for the bakers to get used to all the equipment on board, especially the long deck ovens which stretched back several yards. Then the lorry would tow it to Mykolaiv, while everyone else went by car. There would be two, maybe three days of baking, until all the supplies of flour were used up, with volunteers primed to make deliveries to various villages in Kherson, where plenty of people needed fresh bread. But there are plans, and then there is war, which has no respect for painstaking weeks of logistics and a carefully arranged wall of Post-it notes. First the dough mixer, which had been working happily for many months, decided to choose this moment to expire. Fortunately, there was a spare, a second-hand one which had been on sale for a bargain price. It took a while to install it, which meant no time to do any practice baking on board. Undeterred, the team set off by car, while the lorry began its slower progress along the Mykolaiv road, until suddenly the regular updates from their journey stopped coming. It was getting dark when a photograph finally appeared on the group chat: a stretch of particularly jagged potholes had proved too much, and one of the wheels had completely broken away. By the time they changed the wheel, it was too late to continue and they had to spend the night on the road.

First thing the following morning, after a flurry of 'thumbs up' emojis, they were able to set off for Mykolaiv again. A relieved cheer went up as the lorry rounded the corner into the grounds of a Baptist church, finding a flat piece of grass to park up. The baking team, led by Vlad from Good Bread, drove their van alongside, so that there would be extra space to portion the dough and stack all the tins.

It was unseasonably hot under the spring sunshine, and the bakery ovens were on full blast as the temperature gauge flickered and struggled to reach the necessary 180 degrees. Vlad measured out flour and water, crumbled yeast into the mixer bowl, and turned it on, only to find that something was wrong with the electrics and the machine kept tripping the supply. Every forty seconds it would turn itself off again, while Yurii scrambled to the generator to switch it back on. Various men came to peer at the unfamiliar wiring, until an electrician appeared with a bag of tools and sorted it out. The mixer began kneading properly for a few minutes, until with no warning whatsoever, the sturdy metal dough hook suddenly sheared in half. It seemed as if Sasha's head might explode, but he summoned the electrician again, who conjured up a soldering kit and welded it back together. At last there would be dough, and there would be bread.

It was hot work, manoeuvring the racks of cast-iron tins to the back of the deck ovens, wrestling open the narrow doors without losing too much heat. There was a lot of jostling for space to flip the tins in and out with long wooden paddles which had been specially designed to reach all the way inside. There was just about room to tumble the finished bread onto some cooling racks, the boiling-hot tins grasped firmly with thick oven gloves, before the whole process was repeated again. Vlad had decided to amp up the recipe by adding a mix of dried onion and seeds, and the air grew fragrant with allium and caraway. Finally the finished loaves were slipped into bags, twenty-five of them in each box, stacked neatly in the back of the volunteers' vans. It was well after dark, but not quite curfew; enough time to clean down and lock up, the whirr of the generator finally fading to quiet.

Mykolaiv is still a major city of almost half a million people, which boasts an identical copy of Buckingham Palace in the city centre, inexplicably built in the 1950s to house the local council. It lies at one end of Europe's longest pedestrian street, opposite the regional government offices which were split in two by a missile strike in March 2022. The long pedestrian street was lined with cafes and shops, but with few people around it felt incredibly quiet. There was not much open before eight o'clock in the morning, just a couple of coffee stands serving hot drinks. An intriguing-looking place, the 5th Avenue pop-up, despite a hand-painted sign on the wall declaring 'We Are Working', was closed. A little further along, staff at a small cafe were opening up; it had a few tables on the pavement outside and sold decent coffee and large slices of cake. Despite the early hour, there was cherry crumble pie with ice cream for breakfast. Energy for the road.

The 'Palace of Culture' in the middle of Chornobaivka had clearly seen better days. Before the war there had been school dances there, concerts and children's competitions; now it was all boarded up and had been turned into a hub for humanitarian aid supplies. The Good Bread vans pulled up in the car park beside a long concrete bomb shelter, which was decorated with the cartoon cats the LBWS street art collective had painted all over Odesa and some front-line cities, in an attempt to cheer people up. The three cats were dressed in military uniforms, with machine guns and a Javelin anti-tank missile launcher, smiling in front of a jaunty slogan, 'Good Evening, We Are from Chornobaivka'. Across the square, past the post office, was a free-standing plaque consisting of a large red metal heart with the town's name written across it, which had been reassembled after it was blown apart by a rocket. The volunteers unloaded their boxes of bread onto some old pallets outside the Palace of Culture, along with some lemon cakes and muffins for the children, waiting until a lady from the local council turned up to unlock the doors and ferry everything inside. The Good Bread team drove on into Kherson, where they parked on a nondescript street corner to wait for another local contact. Even during the crippling power cuts, the mobile network has usually managed to operate, and people can stay in touch via apps like Telegram or Signal. Communications get more tricky closer to the front line, when the network is often patchy at best, and the fear of being targeted by Russian drones means volunteers will switch their phones off altogether, or at the very least into airline mode.

There was a little life in Kherson still: Vlad disappeared inside a small grocery shop and emerged with a piece of cake in a cellophane packet, pale-yellow sponge coiled around sweet, thick cream which tasted of warm sugar and a slight aftertaste of dust. A man appeared in a car to lead them through the next blockpost into Antonivka, a town inside the most dangerous red zone, where the bridge across the river led straight to Russian-occupied land. It was a place where no one wanted to linger; it was utterly deserted, as if the streets were silenced under a weighted blanket. The kind of place where you need to drive fast with no seat belt, in case you have to suddenly jump from the car. The irrepressible Dima found time to record a video about the delivery on his phone as they hastily carried the rest of the bread into the local volunteer's house, and then Vlad put his foot down hard on the accelerator and drove straight back to Mykolaiv, relieved that this mission was finally complete.

The last part of the story reads like a detective tale. Sasha and Maria spent weeks scouring endless social media pages and peered at grainy photographs posted online which might reveal if any more mobile bakeries were up for sale. They wanted one to put in the east, and a second to supply communities further south. Finally, it looked as if the detective work had paid off. Zooming in on one of the aerial photos, they could make out what looked like two mobile bakeries in a field outside the city of Uman. Sasha drove straight down there, only to find that they had been completely gutted inside, the bread ovens cut out and reinstalled in a local bakery, marooned behind a concrete wall. It was hard to imagine that any might have survived at all, let alone in a reasonable condition, but the search went on. And then, as that endless hot summer of blackouts wound on, there was a kind of miracle. A friend told them he had discovered two more mobile bakeries, this time relatively intact, sitting in a village near the Belarus border. They were owned by a man from the church who had become a military chaplain. He was willing to give them to Bake for Ukraine free of charge, although they offered to buy him the large generator which he needed to keep the village bakery and shop going during the endless power blackouts. The team went to see the old vehicles, which were rather run down but not entirely beyond repair. There was just the small matter of getting them to Odesa and making them roadworthy again. Another set of challenges waiting for a solution, combined with a good deal of faith.

Part Two

FIRE

HOW TO FEED AN ARMY

Chapter Six
COOKING OVER FIRE WITH MARINES

There can barely be a single Ukrainian family without someone in uniform: almost a million people are currently serving in the armed forces, with more than 150,000 in active combat on the front line. All men aged between eighteen and sixty who are eligible for military service could be called to serve, and although the minimum age for the draft was lowered from twenty-seven to twenty-five, there has been pressure to lower it still further. Mobilisation remains an issue which could hardly be more fraught: how to keep critical jobs going, how to give people sufficient training, how to offer exhausted but experienced soldiers an end date to their service, how to persuade reluctant people to go to war. And just as important are military planning and logistics, including the distinctly unglamorous task of keeping those million soldiers healthy and fed. I was keen to see how it worked in practice.

To reach the village where men from an elite marine battalion have set up their temporary home, you must first find the car park behind a DIY store on the edge of a small town. There, a military press officer will meet you; he takes the front seat in the car to guide the way. You drive past small houses and low-rise blocks of flats, some of them reduced to rubble by Russian shelling. After a while you will stop at the edge of a field where another car is waiting; you will follow it down dusty roads to the destination. Marines move locations a lot. The unit we are visiting say they've stayed in more than twenty different places since the start of the full-scale war. Their battalion has been fighting in the hottest parts of the front line: they were given a special award 'for courage and bravery' by President Zelenskyy for helping to liberate much of Donetsk and Kherson regions. Almost two years into the war, they had been deployed south to make raids across to the left bank of the Dnipro, in the face of what must have been a terrifying onslaught by Russian forces. They have managed to hold on; their motto is 'We are where we are needed.'

While they are on rotation, the men are staying in a number of cottages in a village which must remind them of the farming region they come from in south-west Ukraine. Marines have a reputation for befriending a lot of pets, but I didn't expect to find out that they had adopted a small flock of sheep, in an outhouse at the back of the garden. One of the marines rattles a bucket with some potato peelings inside. 'This is a show, just for you,' he says. 'A performance!' All of a sudden around six sheep rush out in a group, followed closely by a pair of lambs. They canter briefly into some brush at the edge of the field before venturing back towards the outstretched bucket.

It is one of the first sunny days of spring; the sheep are grazing, while some cats and dogs are lounging about, waiting for signs of food. It seems so tranquil, until you remember the enormous cost. One man tells me about the huge impact on their number over the last two years of war. 'There are just thirty of us left now from those who started with us all that time ago.' Many of the men who are serving now have volunteered or been recently mobilised, some fresh from training in the UK, Germany or Spain. We follow one group who are off to do some training. Dressed in full kit, they pick up their weapons and start running through a line of trenches, practising how to clean the area of enemy combatants. One of the men points at some potatoes which will be tied to drones so the operator can get used to manoeuvring one with a grenade underneath. 'Killer potatoes!' he says. There's a video playing on someone's phone, drones dropping grenades on a line of Russian armoured vehicles, which explode in flames, one by one. This time potatoes, next time for real.

Back at the large cottage which serves as their workspace, a kitchen area is crammed with separate fridges for meat, chicken, eggs and cheese; there are sacks of vegetables, cans and packaged food, crates of apples and jars of pickled cucumbers and peppers sent by family or volunteers. There are a couple of ovens, they have electricity, gas canisters and generators to keep power running, as well as a space to wash dishes, while outside there is a wood-fired stove and a large barbecue grate covering a fire pit dug out of the ground. In charge of the cooking is Ruslan, who spent twenty-six years in the navy as a signalman before retiring. As soon as the full-scale invasion happened, he joined up again. 'I had always dreamed of becoming a cook,' he says, 'so that's what I decided to do. It's something I've always wanted to do, so it's never been a challenge – it is always a real pleasure to cook for everyone.'

Each brigade has a specific unit which is responsible for food support, from storing supplies in warehouses to delivery, with the cost of feeding one soldier working out at just under three pounds a day. 'The military authorities create a menu, and send us all the produce we need to make it. As you can see, there is plenty of everything,' Ruslan says: 'Our marines need around 3,500 calories a day, more even than infantry, because we are very active.' There are bags of meals ready to eat, or MREs, neatly stacked in one room, ready for combat assignments when conditions are very different – as well as frozen portions of ready-made food which they can heat up quickly in the microwave. There are even a few packages from the UK. Ruslan said he cooks for around a hundred people at a time, with a couple of men to help. For breakfast that day they had made burgers, while the lunch menu was far more elaborate than you might imagine. They prepared borsch, devilled eggs stuffed with fried onion and mushrooms, trays of meatballs and what Ruslan described as 'field pizza': toasted bread topped with a mix of minced beef, tomatoes and herbs. On the table there are fried pancakes wrapped around hot-dog sausages, and toasted rye bread with garlic and cheese, with more meat sandwiched inside. I ask if they've ever had to cater for a vegan or vegetarian soldier and everyone laughs. 'This is not our tradition. No. We need meat for fighting.'

We go back outside, where some large pans of soup and potatoes are on the grill. 'We can get through ten kilograms of potatoes in one go, it depends how many people we are feeding.' When the food is ready it gets packed into a van and driven to various locations, where the troops file up with their mess tins to collect their lunch. For obvious reasons they don't gather in large numbers in one place, but for a few minutes at least, a few of them can sit around a table and eat together. 'Food is really important to them. Sometimes I think they're like children, they just want sweets – but it's better to give them something that is hot and nutritious,' Ruslan says. 'I had a great cooking tradition in my family, and these are all dishes which I grew up with – so I learned how to make them for the others.' Sometimes, on holidays like Easter or New Year, military cooks even manage to come up with special festive dishes, like Olivier salad made from finely diced potato, carrot, gherkin and mayonnaise, or *kholodets*, a layered dish of shredded meat set in a bouillon jelly.

The marine unit's deputy commander, with the call sign Tamada, comes over – a young man who's been serving for a year and wears a revolver in a holster strapped to his leg. His favourite food, he says, is Ukrainian borsch – and of course the ever-popular meatballs. 'The commander of our whole brigade came here and couldn't believe how good the food was. It shows how we try to do the best for our soldiers and keep them happy.' Even when they are at their positions on the zero line. 'We take dry food and cigarettes; those are the most important things. But sometimes we use drones to deliver food to the left bank [the area on the other side of the Dnipro river which is occupied by Russia]. The first time that happened it was a real shock to have a proper meal at the positions – *varenyky* dumplings, meatballs – that really was a surprise.' Sometimes there's a field kitchen a few miles back from the zero line where soldiers can collect food and hot water for thermos flasks. The more basic the conditions, the less they can cook, so mostly they pack whatever dry rations they can cram into the limited space left in a backpack. I ask Tamada what his call sign means: it translates as toastmaster, after the job he did in his former civilian life. He jokes that his mother had called a few weeks back, to ask if by any chance he was free the following Saturday, as there was a job going at a wedding. These men probably only manage to see their families for a handful of days every year.

'You want borsch? Tea, coffee?' In a narrow kitchen in one of the cottages, a table is set for lunch. The dogs and cats have turned up again in the hope of leftovers, and someone brings out a plate of meat for the animals while we squeeze around the table inside. The borsch is rich and full of vegetables and very good indeed; it's easy to see why Ruslan has built up a reputation for his cooking skills. The men pull out a jar of pickles and some salty sheep's cheese from their native Bessarabia region. 'Our local *brinza* cheese. It is really good.' There is even a waffle cake, layered with thin slices of orange and a thick caramel cream. I had wondered to myself whether it was trivial and ridiculous to talk to men who literally fight for their lives about something as basic and simple as food. But around this table, passing round plates of soup, reaching for some bread, the meal provides a few moments away from the constant stress of war.

One man tells me about their time in Donetsk region during the previous year, when they were fighting around Soledar and Bakhmut, in an industrial mining landscape which was a world away from the rural villages here in the south. 'There has been a lot of Russian propaganda there and the mentality of people is different; many of them have never been anywhere else, they've never been to Kyiv, some of them still look to the Russian direction. It makes you wonder sometimes, why am I defending this territory if people don't want us here?' But then he describes a conversation with a woman who rushed up to them in Bakhmut. 'She said how glad she was to see us there, how happy she was to see Ukrainian soldiers defending her city. And after this conversation I thought, OK, I am ready to defend Donetsk oblast, even if it is just for this woman. Because she is not alone.'

Vlad, a thirty-year-old restaurant chef from Odesa, has been stationed at the front line in Donetsk region for almost a year as an army cook. When the full-scale invasion broke out he had escaped with his family from the city to a small town in Bessarabia region. There they created a small shelter in a basement where people could hide from bombing. 'But I was the only man there, which made me feel uncomfortable. So, I went to the "*Voenkomat*" – the military recruitment centre – and I have been serving ever since.' For a year and a half he was assigned to the *Voenkomat*, and then in mid-2023, he was chosen to join one of the newly created assault brigades as a storm trooper. 'Arriving at the front line is a very scary experience for a former civilian person,' he tells me. 'When I got there, I suggested that I could help out in the kitchen. I was ready to do both: to fight and to cook for those who fight. But they were glad to have me working in the role of chef.' Conditions on the zero line were challenging to say the least. They had no access to water and had to build everything from scratch. Vlad managed to get some help from his former colleagues in the restaurant industry who rallied round and sent some kitchen equipment which he could use. He gathered a small team of fellow soldiers and taught them some cooking skills, as well as how to store and handle food correctly – the basic rules of kitchen hygiene. 'We even managed to get hold of the different-coloured chopping boards you use for different products. And I taught my team how to cook safely – I made it my top priority. Because we had no right to make anyone sick, even though the conditions were very far from a professional kitchen.'

Like Ruslan, his other priority was to provide some feeling of home, for men who spend eight, twelve, sixteen months away from their families. '"It's like home" was the biggest compliment I could get,' he says. 'The kitchen often seems like a warm and soulful place – we don't just cook, we are providing much more.' He describes the set-up he works in as the 'minimum acceptable conditions'. In a place where locations could be suddenly changed at any time, there is little point in creating anything more permanent. 'At any moment this kitchen could be destroyed by a bomb.' They had to be constantly ready to cook for soldiers who could come back from their positions at any time of the day or night.

Even at the front, Vlad insisted that there had been no shortage of supplies: he said he was sent plenty of vegetables, potatoes, all kinds of meat and fish, apples and even bananas. Ukraine's legendary postal delivery service Nova Poshta has remained able to bring packages from home, or whatever extras someone has ordered by mail. The biggest problem has been maintaining a fresh water supply, but Vlad said he was most proud of the fact that he had managed to keep providing his unit with three solid meals a day. I asked about a typical menu. For breakfast, he makes porridge, eggs or sandwiches, while dinner involves some soup, either borsch or *solyanka* – a tomato-based soup with smoked meat – or chicken broth with noodles, followed by stewed meat with potatoes or pasta. And fresh vegetables: 'There is always a salad!' He says soldiers' food, however basic, should give them something to look forward to, and it plays a huge role in morale: 'I can proudly say that when I joined this battalion the lives of the soldiers did change for the better,' adding that he gets plenty of positive feedback to confirm it. Care packages from volunteers are a bonus: 'And it's nice to have someone else cook a meal instead of me, because at some point it does get really hard, cooking three meals a day without time off. We work basically twenty-four hours a day, because sometimes we have to get up at two or three in the morning, to feed soldiers who've just turned up from the zero line.'

But the most difficult thing, of course, is when they don't come back at all. 'The hardest time is when your friend doesn't come back from their military task, or if they are wounded. It's hard to be far from my son. It's hard to find what to be happy about.'

Feeding this million-strong army has not been without controversy. There have been highly publicised scandals over procurement, embezzlement and corruption, while some commanders, one combat medic friend tells me, are far less caring towards the troops in their care. 'Our food was more like buckwheat porridge three times a day,' he says. But then you also see marines taking care of a small flock of sheep and two lambs, a navy veteran who came out of retirement to live his childhood dream of becoming a chef. You read the wall of messages pinned up in the Kulynychi bakery shop on the main road out of Donetsk region, from soldiers thanking the staff: 'Super fantastic!' 'Very tasty, just like home!' 'Awesome place!' You hear about the field kitchen built from scratch, by hand, in an active combat zone, and drones dropping a payload of *varenyky* dumplings. Soldiers cooking over fire, and cooking under fire. Amid so much violence and trauma, they still take every opportunity to find some home comforts and even make the odd cake. As for the future, there is one hope which they all share. 'I dream for the war to be over,' Vlad says.

Chapter Seven

'WHEREVER, FRIENDS' – CHEFFING ON THE FRONT LINE

'Wow, this really is like a restaurant!' the young soldier said, grinning broadly as he packed away boxes of chilled soup, chilli quesadillas and elaborately stacked cheese burgers into the back of his truck. It was late at night after a very long day, and the food, prepared in a field kitchen around thirty miles from Kupyansk by chefs from the Bud De, Druzhe volunteer group, was about to be taken from this lay-by on one of the main highways through Donetsk region, straight to positions on the zero line. Getting it to this point had been a triumph of skill, logistics and meticulous organisation.

'Bud De, Druzhe' which means 'wherever, friend' was born in the early days of the full-scale war, when Alex Maslyanskiy, Valerii Pasichnyk and Yurii Kulyk, three friends who ran a catering company on the left bank of Kyiv, immediately joined the volunteer effort, cooking for soldiers fighting to push back the Russians from the outskirts of the city. At first they made the food at home, then scaled it up in a restaurant kitchen until they were cooking a thousand portions a day for a Special Forces unit. When Kyiv was no longer in imminent danger and the unit was redeployed to the east, they wanted to continue giving practical help. They began developing packs of dried food which could be transported anywhere and cooked with boiling water over a gas burner or small stove. They put their many years of cooking experience into the recipes, coming up with ways to produce dehydrated versions of restaurant-quality dishes like tom yum soup, pasta carbonara and spiced porridge, using the best quality ingredients they could find. Many of the fruits and vegetables came from Valerii's family farm, while they built their own smoker in the yard behind their catering firm to recreate an authentic barbecue taste for the meat. In a converted storeroom, they installed a couple of dehydrators, alongside neatly stacked packs of dried onion, sour cream, mushrooms and several kinds of cheese. They began producing hundreds of thousands of packs of their dried food, tucked into smart blue and silver packaging to match their logo. They somehow fitted in the work after business hours, constantly fundraising to pay for it all, along with posting regular video reports to show what they were getting up to.

As well as sending their food packs through the Nova Poshta delivery service, every few weeks the Bud De team managed to organise their own trips to front-line areas, spending days on the road together to bring freshly cooked food to the units and hospitals that they support. It was a way of reminding their military friends of the times when they used to be able to go to a cafe or out for a meal. 'It all takes time,' Alex explained, when we first met up in Kyiv. 'First we need to earn the money for our fuel and supplies, then we communicate with different brigades to understand where they are – they move a lot and often they rotate with other units. We started our trips with a military hospital near Druzhkivka; we have been there seven times now, and we met many new friends there who we could help in the future.'

The planning which has gone into every one of these trips has been formidable, especially once the Bud De team were all fully employed again, running the catering business and cooking for events. Each time, they had to devise a menu which would be much more appetising than basic rations, but also practical. Sourcing all the ingredients for the right price, deciding what should be prepared in advance and what could be made on location. Working out the equipment to take, what kind of power supply, how to fit everything into the van. Not to mention the challenge of arranging deliveries along a fluid front line where anything and everything could change right up until the last minute. On top of the logistics, each trip has been a hugely emotional experience: Alex says that sometimes they have given food to men just back from days of intense combat. 'Their hands are shaking when they take the plate. Some tell us they haven't been able to eat properly for a week.'

One of the friends they made in Druzhkivka was a former nurse called Iryna, known as Mama Ira. She lived in Chasiv Yar, which by early 2024 had become the latest focus of Russia's offensive. Most of the town had been totally destroyed, including Ira's home. Tears rolled down her face as she described how much she missed it. Even the place where she once went shopping had been wiped out. 'We used to go to the Silpo supermarket in Bakhmut,' she said. 'But now, everything there is gone.' Ira was clearly someone who liked to lead from the front. She moved jobs to manage the catering at another military hospital close to Donetsk region and asked the Bud De team to come and cook there. Their stocks of fresh produce were running short and she wanted the patients and staff to have a day of decent food for a change.

Meanwhile, Alex was also eager to help out a military volunteer unit called Platsdarm. This little-known group is among the war's most unsung heroes, responsible for collecting the bodies of dead soldiers from the battlefield. They carry out meticulous identification, using scraps of personal belongings pulled from the mud or the frozen ground, so that relatives can finally have some closure. They even retrieve the bodies of dead Russians, partly because they believe it is the humane thing to do, but also because Ukraine can then exchange them for its own war dead. It is horrible, unimaginable work, and Bud De wanted to give the Platsdarm volunteers something uplifting for a change. So, plans slowly took shape: cooking for the military hospital, then a day with an assault brigade stationed in the east of Kharkiv region, followed by a series of late-night deliveries into Donetsk region, to hand supplies to various groups of front-line troops. 'We will work some long and hard days,' Alex said. It would be an honour to cook for them, he added, and to spend the whole day with them, rather than just handing out boxes and driving away.

A few weeks later, they were finally ready to set off, beginning the trip in a car park outside the catering company in the suburbs of Kyiv. Their van was packed to the rafters with boxes of ingredients and equipment. There were hotplates and folding tables and huge frying pans, and even a vacuum pack machine; polystyrene cool boxes filled with ice, and huge plastic bottles of a home-made cranberry juice drink called Mors. It seemed incredible that they had managed to stack quite so much inside. Alex sat in front next to his driver friend Denys Iliushchenko, known as Alonso. He had volunteered on highly dangerous missions to evacuate people out of Chernihiv region early in the war, when Russian forces had almost surrounded the area. His father had been killed on one of the missions when his vehicle came under fire, and Denys was the only one who managed to drive back to rescue his body. Valerii took the back seat alongside an older man called Volodymyr Kliuiko, a long-time supporter through his military charity Marinus, collecting many tonnes of vegetables from nearby farmers to donate to the Bud De kitchen. Surrounded by boxes, they set off on the long journey towards the border between Kharkiv and Donetsk regions, the motorway from Poltava giving way to a winding, bumpy road through endless fields and the occasional village.

It was almost dark by the time they pulled up in a town where they had rented two flats to stay for the night, in one of Ukraine's many 1970s-era housing estates, all grey concrete blocks with a view over waste ground and railway tracks. There was tape stretched over the windows to guard against explosions; on closer inspection, the tape was decorated with little smiley faces, and the M&M's logo. A table was quickly laid with pickles and slices of toasted bread, and a paste made from pork fat mixed with herbs and garlic; there were bottles of Ukrainian vodka and fizzy lemonade. Alex made a series of toasts: to the armed forces of Ukraine, to those who had lost their lives, to volunteers, to victory and to Putin's death.

Early the next morning, fuelled by double-strength coffees from a corner grocery shop, they drove through more countryside to the military hospital, the location of which must be kept strictly undisclosed. Mama Ira rushed up to greet them, flinging her arms around Alex, calling him by the familiar diminutive Lyosha, and led the team to the spot outside a small brick building where they could set up their field kitchen. They parked the van next to a large generator and rigged up a power supply. An array of crates and boxes was swiftly unloaded, supplies for the following day were squared away, and Valerii immediately started setting up an outdoor burner and a hotplate – one for toasting hundreds of slices of bread to be sandwiched with the *salo* paste, and one for a wide, curved frying pan, where he would make many portions of potatoes, fried golden brown and crisp with onions and lard. Alex began dicing chicken breast to poach in a smoked cream sauce, and poured large vacuum-packed bags of borsch into catering-sized pans, ready to heat up. Everyone was focused on work: Volodymyr was busy decanting jars of pickled cucumber and tomato onto trays, while Denys toasted slices of dark rye bread on the hotplate. A few soldiers wandered up to see what was happening. They were offered cups of cranberry juice and lard sandwiches, soft cookies filled with poppy seed and apple, and walked away happy. Ira beckoned me inside the hospital: she wanted me to see the place where injured soldiers come straight from the stabilisation point to be treated. One man, with the call sign Gypsy, showed off a long scar down his neck and fished in his pocket for the jagged shard of shrapnel which the doctors had pulled out.

By noon a long queue began forming as soldiers and medical staff arrived for lunch, taking bowls of steaming hot borsch with big spoonfuls of sour cream, and plates of the fried potatoes with chicken and pickles; the lard sandwiches proved especially popular. Ira carried trays of food inside to those who weren't well enough to get out of bed. Other men sat at low benches or crouched on the raised kerbside to eat, smiling and giving the thumbs up sign to show their approval. One man called over: 'Just like home!' The lunch service barely stopped; there were many people to feed: doctors and nurses in their scrubs, men on crutches or with arms in slings. Some leaned on their colleagues for support, others came back for second helpings of soup or bread, exchanging their brigade chevrons with the Bud De cooks in appreciation.

Alex began working on some of the menu for the following day, to get a head start on preparations for the next location – the assault brigade. Among other things, the soldiers would be treated to a summer soup called *okroshka* which includes a lot of finely chopped cucumber, radish, potato and chicken. Volodymyr was sitting beside a seemingly endless pile of boiled potatoes, steadily peeling them and pushing them through a sieve. Once all the vegetables and chicken were prepared, they got mixed with kefir, some water and sour cream and big bunches of dill and wild garlic. The vacuum pack came in handy to seal it all in large bags, stacked between ice cubes to keep fresh until the following day. Finally, as the light faded and the last hospital meal had been served, there was time to wash everything up and pack the temporary kitchen into the van again, a late finish before what Alex warned would be 'another very long and hard day'.

At 5.30 a.m., even the paper cup of corner shop coffee tasted like nectar. The team drove north through the town of Borova and pulled up beside a road where a soldier in a pickup truck was waiting to lead the way to a location close to the edge of Donetsk oblast, in a yard flanked by military vehicles and covered with a camouflage net. 'Everything here has to be finished by 5 p.m.,' Alex declared, 'so from now on, we cannot stop.' It was a slightly surreal experience to be in this location at all, let alone spending the day cooking under a camouflage net.

He had devised an ambitious menu for the brigade: as well as the *okroshka* soup, there would be hot quesadillas and burgers and a fresh cabbage salad with thinly sliced radish, cucumber and dill. It involved a lot of chopping, slicing, assembling salads, grilling buns and packing everything into vac-packs and cardboard containers ready to transport to the east. I had offered to pitch in and help, but soon realised that my skills as an assistant prep chef were significantly lacking, as I chased slippery radishes around the chopping board and wrestled with the intricate origami of the self-assemble burger boxes. By lunchtime, Valerii was busy frying large pans of onions and potatoes again, for they were always in demand. A few soldiers were working at the location, and they got treated to samples of everything. They proclaimed the *okroshka* a big success, sharing bites of quesadilla as well as trying some of the dried food packs destined for troops at the front. Alex thrust one into my hands – a chocolate and hazelnut porridge. 'I don't know when we will eat again, so take this,' he said, giving me a plastic spoon to stir it. The porridge was creamy and delicious, and did not taste like it was made in a foil package with water boiled on a fire, under a canopy of camouflage.

Finally, after a full day of non-stop work, and some last-minute wrestling with fiddly cardboard packaging, everything was cooked and in containers, and the equipment was broken down, cleaned and neatly stacked back into the van. Alex checked his watch: it was just past five o'clock. There was just about time for the obligatory group photo with their military friends before the Bud De team set off, taking the road towards the city of Sloviansk. At the main blockpost, the one just past the big painted Donetsk region sign, festooned with stickers and signatures and flags, Alex pulled over and parked around the back, and walked up to the road to talk to the guards. It was starting to get dark, and on the other side of the checkpoint some soldiers switched on their flashlights to search the back of a van before waving it through. Alex shared a cigarette with one of the men and warned them that he would be driving back late, possibly after the curfew. It didn't seem to be a problem, and he asked if they would all like some freshly cooked cheeseburgers with spicy mayonnaise and onion jam. He didn't have to ask twice. As he ran back to hand out the still warm cardboard boxes, the blockpost guards broke into happy smiles: this had clearly made their night.

It was getting darker by the time the chefs pulled up north of Sloviansk, beside a lit-up sign advertising a long-closed leisure centre where families once went to sail boats and go swimming in a reservoir. They waited around a few minutes before Oleksii Yukov, one of the commanders from the Platsdarm search group arrived – a thin, intense-looking man who must carry the weight of the world on his shoulders. They loaded food boxes into his car, while he smoked a series of cigarettes one after the other and told some traumatic stories about the mission he had been working with since the start of the Russian invasion in 2014. I could not make out most of it, but it involved braving heavy artillery shelling and mines to retrieve bodies, and what sounded like an impossibly difficult task to identify them. 'Many emotions,' said Valerii, as he climbed back into the van, 'and such hard stories.'

We drove on in silence to the next stop in Druzhkivka, nearer to the fighting around Chasiv Yar. 'How far are we from the front line?' someone asked. 'Not too close. Maybe twenty miles.' In the pitch black of a deserted driveway on the edge of town, some young soldiers in combat fatigues were waiting. They ferried boxes into their truck, balancing the trays of quesadillas on top and cheerfully accepted some burgers for the road. They got loaded up with plenty of dried food, because as Alex explained, 'From here they will go straight back to their positions, to the zero line.' They shook hands and embraced, and the boys drove away into the night.

There was just one more stop in the town, a last delivery to men who stopped to examine their packages under the glow of headlights. 'What's in this one? Pasta with carbonara? Yes please, can we take some more of these? Any more of those cookies?' There was the exchange of chevrons, the group photo, the gift of a brigade flag which Alex folded carefully, remarking, 'Another one for the wall of our office!' and Bud De's work, for this trip at least, was finally done. There was the muffled sound of an explosion somewhere nearby, and Denys slammed the van doors shut, ready for the long drive back towards Izyum to spend the rest of the night.

It was well past midnight when we arrived at the accommodation, and everyone was exhausted. There was a kettle on the boil, and over a dinner made up from their own dried food ration packs, Alex brought out the vodka to make some final toasts: to the armed forces, to the victims of the latest Russian missile strike and to victory. Valerii started talking about the terrible weeks he spent living under occupation with his family in Chernihiv region at the start of the full-scale war. Everything was closed, so the only food they had was what they kept at home. It was impossible to go outside, he said, because Russian troops were everywhere; they could arrest you or even shoot you. 'I took flour and made a kind of baguette loaf every day. It was really not very good bread, but we didn't have anything else.'

We were sitting in a basement under a bomb-damaged house, and I thought of all the families left broken and traumatised by war, the millions of people separated from their loved ones for years on end. If you had no sense of purpose you might well feel crushed by it. But Valerii and the other volunteers have thrown themselves into work, and they've published some inspirational quotes from each other on their social media: 'Ukraine will win because even after a generation, they [the Russians] failed to break our desire to reach for light and love – and not like them, for darkness and hatred.' Alex echoed that thought, dreaming of a time when there would be no need for trips like this. 'We are for our children and the future, for the light of freedom.'

Chapter Eight

MAGIC FOOD ARMY

The first time I met chef Zhenya Mykhailenko, he took me to a shawarma stand round the back of the Bessarabian market in Kyiv, where he ordered large, messy wraps filled with chicken, salad and lots of tahini sauce. The second time was over giant bowls of ramen at one of his restaurants in the city. I wondered if I was destined to speak to him only while trying not to spill large amounts of food down my front. Chef Zhenya, as he calls himself on social media, has won a large following, as well as a reputation for his outspoken views. His arms are covered in extravagant tattoos: plants and herbs drawn by his artist wife Mary. As well as running seven restaurants in Kyiv, he has been cooking for Special Forces soldiers since the start of the full-scale war. The couple currently spend their time driving back and forth between Zaporizhzhya, where the military kitchen is based, and Kyiv, where Zhenya still looks after his group of ramen places. Through his Magic Food Army charity, he has assembled a team of cooks who make and distribute thousands of meals for soldiers along the front line. And more than that, he is on a mission to change the way that the entire military food system is organised.

'It was never really a plan,' he says. 'I woke up on February 24th and the Russians were invading our country from all sides. I made the executive decision not to panic and not to leave, because it's my home town. So I went down to one of my ramen shops and told everyone to open on schedule. But by lunchtime we only had sixteen customers, when usually we would have around a thousand. It was pretty obvious that my plan to stay in business wasn't going to happen. I had to come up with a plan B.'

Mykhailenko studied in the United States, taking a diploma in culinary arts at a city college in California, and then returned to his Kyiv home in 2014. He joined the pro-democracy protests in Maidan Square and started helping out with veteran rehabilitation schemes. 'I had been working with military veterans ever since that time, which meant that I had plenty of contacts with different units. The day after the full-scale invasion, I gathered up all my staff, everyone who had not left the country, in my basement kitchen.' There was no shortage of need: he got more than a hundred thousand requests for emergency food assistance a day after posting online, far too many to cope with. They made a decision to focus on soldiers, from a kitchen which was in the heart of the most heavily defended part of the capital, near the government buildings and the presidential palace. 'There were two military academies there, at least three military facilities – it is the safest spot in Ukraine.' Like many other restaurateurs, he began cooking for the troops who had rushed to the defence of the city. It was often unexpectedly lavish. 'We had just done our weekly food purchase on the Tuesday, and the Russians invaded on the Wednesday. We had an entire walk-in larder of food, probably most other places were in the same position. For the first few weeks of the war, everybody ate like kings. We sent out Spanish ham, all sorts of cheese, things like French toast. It was ridiculous.'

By April, he says, when it was clear that the Russians had been chased out of the Kyiv region, he began opening up his ramen shops again. But it wasn't enough. 'It was obvious that we needed to do more. I had a food truck, so I took my wife and one of my drivers and we got into the truck and drove south.' They drove straight to a front-line area where one of the military units they had been supporting in Kyiv had been redeployed. He won't tell me the exact unit, because it's part of the Special Forces, but it did mean that they had not been designed to be a mobile fighting force. 'They had horrible supply logistics. They didn't have a food budget. I stepped up and organised everything, and we went from one unit to the entire battalion along the front line.'

He realised that cooking for men involved in active combat required a deep and practical understanding of their needs. 'In the trenches, their top priority is not food. You don't have time and you're not in the mood to eat when everything is falling around you. But further away from the front, you get people like drone operators, they need to stay awake and be safe. There's a lot of sitting and waiting, but they have to stay alert and keep focusing. So they need to be fed properly.' He wanted the menu to be based around nutrition rather than calories and cost. A proper balance of protein, good-quality fruit and vegetables and slow-release carbohydrates, rather than resorting to energy drinks and chocolate bars. Just as important, he says, is having an infrastructure in place which makes the military food system both efficient and sustainable. 'It was clear we are not going to be doing this for a month. We're going to be doing this for years, and the sooner we realise that, the better.'

The current system is run by a central department at the Defence Ministry. 'They have this daily calorie requirement, and a list of foods which the military can order to meet that requirement. But it assumes that our military also has the technical competence and capacity to actually cook these ingredients. The government thinks the biggest problem is procurement, that the purchasing is corrupt. But whatever they purchase, nobody is thinking about whether the army has a place to store it or to prepare it. They are looking at the wrong problem.' He says it was all rooted in the old Soviet system where everything was centralised and lacked any kind of training in modern, efficient food-preparation skills. Mykhailenko thought his blueprint showed a better way of working. 'We had engineers who came up with a solution, one that could work along the entire 900 kilometres of the front line. There would be refrigerated hubs, we fill them up with food, guys come from their positions, pick up what they need and take it back there, meals prepared in a way which would mean they last for five days or even up to a week without being packed full of preservatives.'

He says a background of classical technique and cooking for thousands of people at a time when he worked in Los Angeles had stood him in good stead. 'I started with classic Italian, and classic French and if you mix that with my background in large-scale operations, I brought all that with me when I started to cook ramen in Kyiv.' Ramen, he says, is a deceptively simple dish that takes a huge amount of knowledge to get right. 'It looks easy on the surface, but the amount of work that goes into every ingredient in that bowl is quite ridiculous. How much you can obsess about making your bowl perfect.' He is also a fan of running a military-style brigade system in his kitchen, which he has decided is the only way to operate so close to the front line. 'We are basically working about forty kilometres from the trenches, so we are very close. For many months, we were living together with the military staff, which was kind of putting us in danger. So we needed to impose some discipline, while it helped us to understand exactly what the military needs. And since I worked in large-scale food production I know how to achieve that kind of emergency logistics. I wouldn't know how to transport an Abrams tank but I do know how to transport pork carcasses, how to break them down, how to turn them into cutlets, and how to make them keep safely for five days at a time.'

I had asked if it would be possible to visit the Zaporizhzhya kitchen to see it at work, but at the time, it was in a highly restricted location and completely out of bounds. Instead we looked at a laptop as he talked me through some floor plans and videos which he had taken walking around the kitchen space. The layout had been carefully planned to incorporate separate spaces for storage, packing and cleaning. His watchwords were clearly hygiene, quality control and efficiency; the place looked pristine and he wasn't shy of expressing some strong feelings about the kind of volunteer kitchen operations where people peeled stacks of vegetables over buckets on the floor. He had invested hundreds of thousands of dollars on high-tech kitchen equipment to take care of the basic tasks, and blast cooling technology to shock freeze the packaged meals so that they could be stored safely without spoiling. 'We make sure all the food is down to five degrees Celsius as quickly as possible. Once the ingredients are cooled, the portioning team comes in, goes into the cooler room and boxes it up, while it remains between two and five degrees. Then we drive to a logistics hub on the front line which has a refrigerator room. Then it moves to wherever the units are. Food moves at two Celsius throughout the entire supply chain. Because of that, we are able to make properly nutritious meals: salads, seafood, yoghurt, everything they need for proper nutrition.'

He shows me the way they pack food in layers to make sure it lasts. A salad, for example, has the heavier and wetter ingredients at the bottom and a layer of sour cream on the top to keep it airtight: 'Nature's cling film.' Inside the cold room where all the meals are assembled, the cooks are dressed in thick jackets and fleece hats, as they carefully weigh out all the separate components into their individual plastic trays. A typical day's work might involve packing more than two thousand ready-meals and delivering them along a logistics route which can run more than a thousand miles. I asked what kind of meals they typically provide: there are dishes like *sous vide* chicken with buckwheat and mixed vegetables, pancakes filled with fruit and curd cheese, or borsch and home-made bread, baked in the steam convection oven. Mykhailenko wants to buy ingredients at scale, but he also gets a lot of his quality produce from an American farmer called Helen, who has been running an organic farm about 180 kilometres from Kyiv for the last twenty years. She counted many expats and the US embassy among her customers, and donated a lot of fruit and vegetables to his Magic Food Army, free of charge. 'Lucky me!' he says.

We took a walk around his Kyiv headquarters, in the building above the ramen bar. There are bedrooms where staff can stay, as he still takes on a few volunteers from overseas. There's a display of military memorabilia from the front, shell cases and bits of abandoned Russian uniform pinned to the walls. In the common room, there are bean bags to sit on. It is unexpectedly Zen and calm. 'Only World Central Kitchen has managed to keep going purely with volunteers. You can't expect volunteers to build their lives around this kind of work into the long term. That's why we started hiring people and paying them, because we understood this wasn't going to be a part-time job.' He is planning to show what he has built to the Defence Ministry, in the hope that they will take on the idea, and scale it up from his current donation-based model. 'As I said, the problem doesn't lie in purchasing food,' Mikhailenko says. 'The problem is what happens after that. My system provides the soldier or an officer with a complete portion of food and all they need to do is keep it stored and heat it up. If you give a soldier a bunch of food that he needs to cook, that presents most of them with a whole lot of challenges that they don't need.'

He has spent two years trying to solve that problem, in the most professional and modern way possible. 'They still use these horrible thermoses from the 1950s. To deliver food you still need a kitchen and somewhere to store food at cold temperatures. They are trying to play by the book because they don't know any better.' He wants to effectively contract the meal system out, away from those whose specialism has nothing to do with cooking or food, although he wants to stay in control of the whole process. 'I report directly to the general. There's no one higher up than the commander. So I speak mostly with them and plan for our operations. I often just do surveillance; I monitor how the operation works. So sometimes I just hop on the side seat with the driver and go along the front line and check what's going on. That's the best way to find out where everyone is. They want to make me believe that everything is fine. But every time I drive by I find some faults. Maybe then I will fire someone.'

He talks about the lack of training, and a Ukrainian education system which doesn't yet have the resources to bring on enough new cooks. 'If you're willing to work, I'm willing to teach you. Sometimes you need to clean out the freezer or spend a whole day butchering pork carcasses, turning them into schnitzels or meatballs. But I am willing to show you how to turn this into something that will allow you to make your livelihood with your own two hands.' The kind of skills, he said, which stood him in good stead when he first moved to the United States. 'I worked with Mexicans, and I didn't speak any Spanish. But I realised that the only language of the kitchen is how you move and how fast you can do tasks.' He compares his profession to a martial art. 'People are always saying chefs are artists, but it is a very specific kind of art. You need to repeat things to the same standard, you need to be tough. You have to endure physical work for many hours. It's not like picking up a paintbrush.'

We had arranged another meeting, but late the night before, I got a text message. There had been some kind of security breach at the base, and he and Mary had to suddenly rush back to Zaporizhzhya and start moving the entire kitchen to another location across the city, as quickly as possible. 'Change of plans,' read the message. 'Evacuating now.' They had only just installed it – a process which had taken many weeks of hard work. I messaged back the next day to ask how things were going. 'Still dismantling equipment. So far so good!'

A couple of months later Mary, Mykhailenko and I set off on the six-hour drive south to see the new kitchen in Zaporizhzhya, a mainly industrial city around thirty miles from Russian-occupied territory. It was already late evening as we approached the blockpost on the outskirts of the city, but it was still possible to make out the giant chimneys which dominated the skyline, and the unmistakable odour of sulphur mixed with smoke. 'Welcome to Zaporizhzhya,' Zhenya said. 'You can smell it already.' The streets were mostly empty and shrouded in the familiar darkness of all Ukrainian cities so close to the front line. 'That is the hotel which was bombed,' Zhenya said, pointing at a circular concrete building on the edge of the riverbank as we drove past. It had been popular with aid workers and the United Nations, but it was badly damaged by a direct missile strike in the summer of 2023. 'And the hydroelectric dam, they bombed it in March. It was like Swiss cheese, full of holes. You can see where it is still being repaired.' As we drove across the dam, an air alarm came on, warning of glide bombs. 'Welcome to Zaporizhzhya,' Zhenya said again, scanning the horizon for any evidence of 'arrivals', a word which fast became part of Ukraine's wartime vernacular to refer to incoming attacks.

We reached the kitchen without incident, pulling up in a large car park behind a building which was missing a large part of its roof. Inside, there was a huge amount of space which had been divided into a main kitchen area and various types of storage, including freezers and a cold room, where carefully weighed-out portions would be packaged up for delivery. There were pictures of his favourite chefs up on the walls, the Ukrainian and EU flags, and some basic recipes for things like sauces and stocks, written in marker pen straight onto the tiles. There was also a mountain of bottled water, and a powerful generator, capable of keeping the place running during blackouts. Zhenya pulled out a couple of boxes of the meals which the troops would be getting, so that we could heat them up for dinner back at his house. There was even a cake – a chocolate muffin topped with cream cheese frosting. It was a generous portion of food: breaded chicken breast, with mashed potato and several kinds of vegetables, including broccoli cooked with ginger and garlic. 'They are always overcooking the broccoli,' Zhenya said, jabbing at the plate with his fork. 'I guess I will have to show them again how to make it properly.'

The next morning, we drove back to the kitchen in time for a morning briefing, over a staff breakfast of pancakes with cottage cheese and jam, and a fresh fruit salad, another meal the soldiers would be having in their next delivery. While Zhenya began building the following week's menu and doing costings on his laptop, each section got down to work, under the watchful eye of that day's head chef, a quietly efficient man called Vova. In the main kitchen, two cooks were putting on huge pans of water for buckwheat and potatoes, while Daniel, a chef who had recently joined the team from Boston, was busy breadcrumbing hundreds of pork fillets, ready to go in the deep fryer. Everyone wore different-coloured aprons denoting their seniority in the kitchen; they had all been given military ranks, and Daniel was in training to become an officer, so that he could take charge of looking after other international volunteers. In another room, a group of women cooks were busy preparing vegetables for salads and soups. Alongside two local women, both called Natalia, there was Donna, a retired teacher from Canada, who was tackling a huge pile of root ginger and fresh herbs. They worked long hours, she told me: a van would typically come to pick them up for the early shift at around five thirty in the morning. They finished when every job that needed doing was done. One of the Natalias was learning how to use some new equipment designed to chop large amounts of vegetables at once. It had been a substantial investment, several thousand dollars, but Zhenya was adamant that it would save a huge amount of time and effort in the long run. Back in the main kitchen, he was showing Vova how to make the broccoli side dish, stirring constantly at a huge frying pan full of grated ginger, moving it about over a high heat until the water evaporated away and it began to caramelise. 'Now add the garlic,' he said, 'and be very careful because it will burn.'

One of the cooks brought over a tray of cooked broccoli which had been cooling down in the fridge, and Zhenya poured over the sizzling garlic and ginger mixture until it coated everything. Then he lit up a blowtorch and began charring it; there was a lot of attention to detail for a single side dish. Zhenya said that every time he cooked a dish, he imagined the soldier who would be eating it. Nothing but perfection was good enough.

Across the corridor, a room full of crates was waiting. They were stacked in different colours, each for a separate destination along the 900-kilometre front line, so that the drivers would know where to deliver them. They would be driven to places like Kupyansk, Orikhiv, Pokrovsk and Kherson, filled with carefully prepared food, portioned out by hand in the chiller room by cooks wearing puffa jackets and gloves, and vacuum-sealed at a low temperature designed to keep without spoiling for several days. Mary pulled out some of the beautiful labels she had created for each box with a drawing of the contents, along with all the nutritional information about the meal contained inside. There would be hours of work ahead to portion out the meals and pack the crates, so they could be dropped off at prearranged spots which are constantly changing for security reasons. There were thousands of pancakes, folded around cottage cheese, nestled neatly into their trays with jam and chopped fruit on the side. Daniel, the chef from Boston, was working through his mountain of pork fillets, each one fried crisp before being chilled, then boxed up with buckwheat and the garlicky-gingery seared broccoli which they had just been learning how to make. There was even freshly baked bread, expertly made by one of the local women, who was also a skilled baker.

There can't be many front-line soldiers who regularly get food as good as this. But that is what drives Zhenya

Mykhailenko onwards: he wants to feed his units better, to feed the armed forces better, to feed Ukraine better. Two and a half years into the full-scale invasion, they had prepared around a million portions of food, and launched a new fundraising drive to buy even more equipment so that they could double their capacity. They had plans to source a modular kitchen, similar to those used by the American army, to enable better cooking facilities for troops in firing positions on the front line. At the time of writing, the Ukrainian Defence Ministry had recalled hundreds of millions of tonnes of military food because it failed to meet quality standards. Zhenya and his Magic Food Army firmly believe that their way of working would make that kind of scandal a thing of the past.

Chapter Nine
NATALIA'S VOLUNTEER KITCHEN

During the long winter of 2022, it seemed perpetually cold and dark. Ukraine had been plunged into blackouts and energy cuts after Russia bombed power stations and put critical infrastructure out of action. That December, I had decided to find out how Ukrainian volunteer groups managed to deliver supplies to front-line areas on such a regular basis, and do more to amplify their stories. I met up with Dmytro, the young drummer with the Ukrainian pop group Antytila, who helped to run their charity arm. He was leading one of their regular delivery runs from Kyiv to the east, which involved a journey of almost a thousand miles crammed into just two days. It was an incredible insight into the risks, the tenacity and the sheer determination that it all involved. One of the volunteers I met was a woman called Natalia who ran a twenty-four-hour kitchen which had never stopped working since the first day of war. She was so inspiring that I immediately thought: her story deserves to be told.

The Antytila foundation team had planned a route down through Donetsk region to drop off food, generators and encrypted radios to the territorial defence units which they supported. There had been the chance to catch just a few hours sleep during the first night, on the floor of a former holiday chalet deep in the forest. It had become home to soldiers who stayed there between rotations, somewhere between Lyman and Sloviansk. In the morning they offered us mugs of sweet, instant coffee, and I noticed that next to the kettle there was an unexpected jar of jam from the British supermarket Asda. There wasn't much else in the way of food, but towards the end of the second evening, after fifteen hours of non-stop deliveries, Dmytro wanted to make a last drop at a place which repaired military vehicles and repurposed captured Russian tanks. After that, he promised, we would drive to a volunteer canteen.

The inky darkness of blackout made it hard to see very much, and for safety reasons any outward sign of the canteen was hidden from view. But everyone who has taken that road through the Dnipropetrovsk region knows about the place: a haven of warmth and hospitality in a place where everything around seems broken and cold. We walked inside, blinking in the half-light of the front yard, where some huge pans of soup were simmering away on a row of wood-fired stoves. We passed a tap rigged up by the wall so that people could wash their hands, before we went into the main room, bright and welcoming, walls covered with signed flags and brigade chevrons from grateful guests and supporters. Along one side were boxes filled with donated bread, fruit and vegetables and many jars of pickles. But the room was dominated by a huge, long table, flanked with chairs and loaded with jugs of fruit juice and all kinds of food. A bus pulled up outside, carrying soldiers from a nearby hospital. They filed in and sat down at one end, while some paramedics had a quick cigarette outside before joining them. A young woman carried bowls of steaming hot soup to the table; there were plates of potato salad, filled pancakes, cured meat and pickles, while dishes were replenished as soon as they were finished. It was an astonishing sight.

We were urged to take a place and have some soup: the borsch was incredible and tasted both homely and instantly comforting. One of the soldiers saw me taking a photo of the meal on my phone and laughed, pulling out his phone to show me the smashed-up screen. He had been carrying it in a kit bag when it was hit by a bullet, he said, gesturing to the place under his arm where it had been. Fortunately, he had not been badly injured, but the phone was definitely a thing of the past.

I really wanted to do something to thank the women who ran the kitchen and were doing such a remarkable job. Under lamps powered by a generator, Natalia showed me around the area where they managed to prepare and cook food for hundreds of people every day. I asked if there was anything they needed. 'We could use a big blender, because sometimes men who've been injured come here, and they can only manage to eat soup,' she said. A few days later, thanks to the help of a chef friend who managed to find the right kind of professional blender for sale and even negotiated a discount, we had one delivered to the kitchen. Natalia sent back a photograph, taken in front of the brigade chevrons: she was dressed in a khaki fleece top with the word 'Volunteer' on a patch across her front, wielding the massive blender like a weapon.

Just over a year later, in early 2024, when I had taken a sabbatical from working in the newsroom to spend a far longer period in Ukraine, I made another trip to the kitchen. I arranged a lift with a Ukrainian colleague called Yevhen, who I had met up with in Kharkiv. 'Are you sure they are still open?' he had asked. 'So many of these volunteer places have not managed to keep going after such a long time of war.' The kitchen was indeed open, serving anyone who turned up – twenty-four hours a day, seven days a week. Before the war

Natalia had been running a shop and small cafe, and as soon as the full-scale invasion happened there were huge convoys of Ukrainian troops driving past, heading towards the front lines in the east. They began stopping at her shop to buy supplies, and asking for hot coffee. She began making some simple food, serving it up on the roadside.

We caught up with her outside, snug against the chilly morning in her trademark fleece. 'On the 24th, maybe the 25th of February 2022 a bus of soldiers turned up. I gave them coffee and some pies to take with them, because they didn't have time to stop. But they were asking about soup and if we had any borsch; they said they had no time but they really wanted to try it. So then we decided to cook it in advance, so that we would always be ready for anyone just to jump in and take some soup. We created this volunteer kitchen, and we've been running it like this ever since.' No one is ever turned away. 'Usually we have around two thousand people a day coming through. On the busiest days it can be three and a half thousand.' Like so much of Ukraine's volunteer economy, it is completely funded by donations and the generosity of friends and supporters.

I had brought a gift, an enormous jar of pickled cucumbers which had been given to me by an elderly *babusia* who I had visited with a charity near Izyum the day before. I put it down next to hundreds of other donated jars of pickles stacked outside, where it looked very much at home. A delivery of cabbages and potatoes had just arrived. 'We have a big network of friends,' Natalia explained. 'They bring us what they have, a lot of it grown in neighbouring places.' We walked inside, past the row of pots on the wood-fired stoves, and she showed me a small room which they had managed to fit out with a couple of washing machines and a drier, so that soldiers who had spent days covered in mud and dirt would have somewhere to change their clothes. 'The boys were always asking me if there was anywhere where they could clean up. At first we would take the clothes home and wash them there, but it is much easier now we have the machines right here. They can drop it off and pick it up clean and dry in the morning.' Unexpectedly, in the warm space beside the drier, there were a couple of chinchillas sleeping in cages, donated by someone who had rescued them from a house evacuated near the front line.

Inside the main dining area, the walls were completely festooned in brigade flags, while there was barely room to fit any more chevrons alongside. We sat down at one end of the table, which seemed to be laden with an even more lavish spread of food than on my first visit. 'We don't have a fixed schedule, because nothing can be planned,' Natalia said. 'Guests just come by because so many people know about this place. Most of them are soldiers and volunteers so it's always free of charge. We have some displaced people, refugees, anyone who wants to stop and eat something.'

As word spread, they kept getting bigger. 'A lot of people come past here; we are about 120 kilometres from Bakhmut, kind of in the middle of the route from Donetsk region to Dnipro. And there aren't many other options around here.'

She has kept the kitchen running thanks to a large team of around seventy volunteers who take it in turns to look after all the cooking and food preparation, working in shifts around the clock. 'They have a huge amount of empathy for our soldiers, and they want to do something to help them. So, we have to keep on working and giving the opportunity to stay involved.' She lowers her voice and points at one lady, who is silently serving out bowls of soup. 'Her son was serving in the military. He was killed a few months ago. She comes here now from Dnipro, to work every morning. This is how she remembers him. She feels so sad, but she keeps on helping out here, because she lost her son.'

Natalia's own son is serving in the armed forces, while her eighteen-year-old daughter is helping in the kitchen. At one point her husband Anatoly comes over to join us: this is very much a family affair, supported by the whole community. 'Our main challenge is paying for the electricity, because we are constantly sent donations of food and other supplies. We get support from all over Ukraine, from Poltava, from Lviv and especially from Cherkasy because that's where I come from.' She starts telling us a story about a group of men who had come in shortly after the war started and she thought their accents sounded familiar. 'I asked if they were from Cherkasy and they said yes. Later they got back in touch and sent us a lot of necessary supplies.' Often people who just come in for a meal bring some packages of food or cash donations. 'It is really just about hospitality. We don't try to compete with any other places which might be doing the same thing. There is no such thing as competition between volunteers; we just want to unite the whole of Ukraine behind this basic idea.'

All this time, small groups of soldiers have been coming inside, sitting together to eat. A couple of older men take some plates of food, and stop to drop some money in the donation jar on their way out. Natalia organises some bowls of borsch for us, offering some fluffy home-made garlic *pampushky* buns to go with it. 'Ukrainian borsch is definitely the most popular dish we make. It all depends what ingredients we have, we are always having to improvise. So today, we are baking some pies, some sandwiches and potato salad.' She runs through a list of dishes which are usually on rotation: pilaff rice with meat, buckwheat and mashed potatoes, the layered meat and jelly terrine called *kholodets*.

But borsch remains a constant fixture on the menu. 'Some guys came here after about four months of fighting at the front, and we served them this borsch. One of them started crying, and we asked him what was the matter. He told us it was exactly like the one his mother made, and for half a year he hadn't been able to taste a proper borsch. So that's why it is important for us to keep making it.'

Having a big communal table full of sharing food is part of the plan. 'Sometimes people are surprised when they come in to see that there aren't separate tables. It's almost like being at an event. But we wanted it to feel like a big family getting together, and everybody likes that.' It is certainly a way to tackle the sheer loneliness of war, for those who are far from their own families or who have lost everything they knew. But it must be a hugely emotional challenge for anyone who volunteers, especially when they work directly with people heading straight to the front line, or have their own family members involved. 'If not all, almost all of us who work here have someone who is at the front. But giving support, both emotional and practical, this is the most important part. You can't say that "I quit" or "I've had enough." Even when it feels really hard, you keep going because you are exactly where you are needed.'

We pause to eat some food, passing plates of pickled vegetables and salty cheese, and buns filled with apple jam. 'We like to offer the guys moral support and empathy. Sometimes they say it isn't so scary going back to the battlefield if they know someone behind them is really worried about them. Sometimes we just hold their hands, and tell them, "I wish these hands will never get hurt" or something like that. But the most challenging part is when you see them leaving for the front. Of course you are happy when they come back, but when they jump on a bus going that way, it is the hardest.' She tells me about ambulance drivers who come with injured soldiers in the back. 'We have some clothes we can give them, because some of the injured ones have barely any uniform left. So now they can get some spare things from us.'

And so her band of volunteers keeps on working, covering two shifts during the day and another one overnight, including holidays when they try to make some special dishes like Easter *paska* bread or Olivier salad. 'At any moment a bus can just stop and a hundred people are suddenly here. We never have a situation where someone comes in and we can't offer them any food. One pan of borsch is always ready, and the second one is on the go. So many different units come through, the Georgian Legion, Azov. We even had that Russian freedom legion here [a group of anti-Putin Russians who were fighting on the side of Ukraine]. And some Colombians, they were really happy to be here, and came back five times. Every time they kept saying "*Slava Ukraini!*" to us.'

Natalia shows me some TikTok videos she has made of the team, dancing as they cook, and trying to chop wood for the stoves. 'When there are no men around, we chop wood. We take care of it. No one here is a professional cook, but they are professional housewives, there is nothing impossible for them.'

Her husband Anatoly passes around some fruit juice called *uzvar* and she calls up another video on her phone, a song which someone wrote about her after being inspired by her kitchen, and turns up the volume. As the rousing music plays, sitting at this table, filled with so many lovingly prepared plates of food, you can feel the presence of the tens of thousands of people who have eaten here. Young men on their way to battle, exhausted ambulance drivers, emergency workers, volunteers just back from delivering supplies to the front line, soldiers in filthy clothes who get the chance to clean up and have a warm bowl of borsch. Like the military men she looks after, Natalia tells me she has her own call sign: appropriately enough, it is 'Kombat'. 'No one expected us to keep going all this time, but we are still here. And there is no going back.'

Part Three

TIME

A BUSINESS AT WAR

Chapter Ten

KHARKIV OPENINGS

To run a small business in wartime is to master the art of resilience. To open a small business in wartime, in a near front-line city, attacked daily with missiles and drones, where half the population has fled, where windows are boarded up and city landmarks are battered and burned, is taking that resilience to the next level. At the Pakufuda cafe not far from Kharkiv's central Freedom Square, during the intense fighting in the early months of the war, a young baker called Kshu had slept in a storeroom next to the basement bakery which doubled as a bomb shelter, rolling up her mat in the morning to start work. Volunteers at the Myrne Nebo charity bakery had flung themselves under their big metal table to shelter from shelling, emerging when it paused to roll out their dough again. During curfews, during blackouts, postal deliveries still continued. As the months went on, some of the places which had closed began returning to work. And in a stark reminder of the sacrifice of war, a coffee shop was opened by the mother of a soldier in the Kraken Regiment (a high-profile volunteer regiment which took part in the defence of Kharkiv) who was killed at the front. It had been Andrii's dream to open a cafe, so she named it Palomnyk after his call sign, filling the place with photographs of her son along with memorabilia from his brigade.

I had been making regular trips to Kharkiv for almost two years, and businesses had gradually found a way to deal with the challenges of operating during war. The first time I went there, in September 2022, the city centre was lined with boarded-up windows and silent streets, with the occasional notice scrawled outside places which were open: 'We are still working'. But as the Ukrainian counteroffensive that autumn pushed the Russians out of most of Kharkiv region, and out of artillery range of the city, thousands of people began to return home. It was not exactly busy, and too many of its beautiful facades were scarred by bomb damage and shrapnel, but families began walking through the parks on sunny weekends, and cafes, galleries and basement bars brought communities some solace and light. By late 2023, Kharkiv's food scene had become second to none: you could find incredible croissants at Café 1654, filled with salmon and avocado and bunches of fresh herbs. Wood-fired beetroot with salty *brinza* and smashed beans on toasted rye at the effortlessly cool modern Ukrainian restaurant Tripichya. Rows of picture-perfect patisserie at Czukerka; the best sourdough and cardamom buns at Pouhque; every kind of street food at the chic open-air food hall 7 Sklad. They managed such high standards, even when menus had to write 'GEN' next to items they were able to cook off-grid, in a city which was powered only by dogged persistence and diesel generators.

For Boris Lomako, the man behind some of Kharkiv's coolest and most popular food businesses, working even harder became a matter of patriotic duty: 'I want to show that there is life here in Kharkiv,' he said, 'and if there is life here, that it is worth fighting for.' On the very first day of the full-scale invasion, he put his family in the car and drove to Lviv in western Ukraine; they went on to the European

Union, and he immediately drove back the other way, to Kharkiv again. He searched for a basement kitchen where he could safely work with his restaurant team, cooking for military units who were battling to defend key locations like Kharkiv airport and city hospitals. They managed to produce around a thousand meals a day from a kitchen below his shuttered restaurant Gaga, before the site was hit by a rocket fragment and they swiftly relocated to a colleague's kitchen much further from the front lines, in the town of Kamianske in Dnipropetrovsk region. The space was bigger and better equipped, and they worked long hours, turning out three, then four thousand portions of food every day. 'We sealed it all in vacuum packs, so it was really cool for soldiers, they could take any dish like borsch or stuffed cabbage, and store it for as long as four days without needing a fridge.' They made food for thousands of Kharkiv residents who'd been forced to seek refuge in the city's metro network, until by June he realised that soldiers had managed to get their own cooking organised, and residents were slowly going back to their home kitchens. It was time to reopen Gaga as a restaurant; he resolved to keep volunteering, but start doing business again at the same time.

I went to meet Boris Lomako in spring 2024, after that emergency lifestyle had given way to a wartime version of business as usual. We are talking in the construction-site surroundings of his latest restaurant collaboration, a breakfast-led place called Snidanishna, on one of the city's main avenues near the botanical gardens. His previous restaurant, in the city's five-star Palace Hotel, had been completely destroyed just a few weeks earlier when a Russian missile tore into the building. 'For one and a half months the restaurant was open and working, and then it was destroyed.' It took him three days to pay everyone their wages, cover the outstanding costs and then start all over again with Snidanishna. Next-level resilience.

We walk around the half-completed space, stepping carefully around workmen who are installing a bar down the length of the room, the smell of wet concrete hanging in the air. 'This place will be an acknowledgement of love to the city and to Kharkiv's people,' he says. Together with Darya and Mykhailo Lazarev, they had come up with the idea of a casual restaurant serving mainly brunch-style food, with an on-site bakery and space to sell things from a selection of small, artisanal producers from across the region.

The rest of his team, he explains, had gone on a field trip to Opishnia in Poltava region, a town known as the 'pottery capital' of Ukraine, to source some ceramics for the restaurant 'They have their own clay there. Almost in every house, there's somebody making some ceramics from this clay.' On a previous trip, they went north to a small town in the Sumy region, where the lack of railways and large-scale infrastructure meant it had been relatively protected from the iron fist of Soviet influence. 'People there know more about the traditions of their grandparents. We found one woman who makes these special Christmas sweets, kind of stretched candies. You make it by putting a pan of boiling-hot syrup directly on the snow, and then start stretching out the caramel. It fills with air, the structure changes into a long, crunchy sweet. They used to give it to people who turned up singing Christmas songs.' This commitment to Ukrainian heritage is central to the entire project: instead of selling doughnuts which 'everybody does', they will make a local type of dough fritters called *verhuny*, avoiding anything too expensive or flashy, because they understand that tastes are simpler when times are harder. 'It's not like we will just copy things from a hundred years ago; it isn't a museum, it's a business, but we can make these things from our history and traditions cool again.'

It would be hard to find anyone who captures Kharkiv's energy and determination more than Dima Kabanets, who's been running his Makers Coffee business since 2019. In July 2023, after more than a year of full-scale war, he opened a brand-new site in the centre of Kharkiv, as well as a small coffee kiosk in the embattled town of Kupyansk, shelled almost into oblivion by the Russian forces holed up just a few kilometres away. 'We have just one difficulty with this shop, and that is the Russians and their war. We don't really know how many people will come back to Kharkiv, or how many of them will come to our coffee shops. But maybe I do this because if you live in war, if you live in a front-line city, you need something for your heart and for your soul,' he says. Like Boris Lomako, he has been determined to keep providing jobs for the city: he employed five staff members in this new branch and a barista in the front-line town of Kupyansk who was eager to continue working. 'We had been working with a volunteer hub there called Hub Vokzal, they give people warm clothes, help with heating, that sort of thing. So we began thinking about what we could do for the military and people who stay in Kupyansk, so we opened this little kiosk with coffee, and it's the same here in Kharkiv – we work, and we give hope or relief and a place for our baristas and cooks.' One of their staff members had been living in Berlin for a year, where she'd escaped to when the war first started. She had discovered Makers Coffee on social media, and decided to come back to Kharkiv and work there, in the kitchen. 'People message me and say they see what we do, and tell us that if we open places here when the war is really close, it's really cool and it's really brave. But honestly, it's something for my soul.'

But for anyone who lives and works in Kharkiv, the war is never far away. Just a few days into 2024 came a shocking reminder of exactly how close it was to Dima. On the night of January 23rd, two Russian missiles slammed into the centre of Kharkiv, a few yards from Makers Coffee. More than two hundred buildings were damaged, and Dima's flat was just around the corner. 'I was at home with my wife and daughter when the shelling happened, and I felt the explosions on my skin – it was really very scary,' he said. He got a phone message about the coffee shop, and when he opened the video, he could see the window was all broken and things inside were smashed. His first thought was about the emergency crews working at the scene. 'I thought, come on, they need coffee, my coffee, so all night we were making hot drinks for the DSNS state emergency workers, for the ambulance and police; and then a lot of people, my customers and friends, began arriving to help clean up the mess.' The friends, including the well-known Kharkiv street artist Hamlet Zinkivsky, swept up the broken glass and helped to fix up boards where the windows had been, and at eight o'clock the following morning the coffee shop opened as normal again. If anything about the situation could be described as normal. 'After that night when the rockets came, even more people turned up than when we first opened. So many people came to support us that we had a record day for takings!'

Dima posted a video a few days later on the Makers Instagram feed, showing all the people who'd come to help clean up, mixed together with shots taken a month before when the same friends and customers had been helping to put up Christmas lights. He hadn't wanted to post the Christmas footage, he said, at a time when his city was being attacked with such ferocity. But then he realised it was all evidence of his community, of the people who would come and drink coffee or pin up decorations or sweep up the debris of bomb damage on a freezing cold January night. 'I'm not going to leave for another city with my family,' he says. 'My daughter was two months old in February 2022 and now she's two years old and we have been in Kharkiv the whole time.'

Snidanishna were proud of their specialist bakery, and their range of cakes, versions of traditional recipes from different Ukrainian regions: a Lviv cheesecake, a Kyiv cake sandwiched with meringue and rich cream, the jam shortbread cookies often known as 'grated pie', a layered torte from Uzhhorod and Ivano-Frankivsk. The restaurant's co-owner Darya Lazareva fetched the plates which the team bought from the specialist town in Poltava region, a rich brown-coloured glaze with hand-painted flowers. One of the jugs on the table belonged to her husband's grandmother. 'I think we lost this connection to our past around a hundred years ago. In the USSR, Ukrainians were treated as second-class people and their designs were considered ugly. But we want people to see these and think – wow, this is really Ukrainian? It is beautiful and I want to touch it. It makes me proud.'

We tried several kinds of bread, including a soft, fragrant loaf made with dark rye and another with buckwheat, spread liberally with local butter mixed with wild garlic and salt – everything was excellent. The next day, when the kitchen had opened at full capacity again, I tried a dish called *gombovtsi*, from the Zakarpattia region: pillowy curd cheese dumplings rolled in light crumbs, with a cherry inside, served in a pool of sour cherry compote, which is as delicious as it sounds. Despite enormous problems with electricity after Russia completely destroyed the thermal power plant which kept the city supplied, Snidanishna has stayed open with a generator and a wood- fired oven, developing new dishes for the menu to keep up with the changing seasonal produce. Boris Lomako put on a three-day workshop to mentor other Kharkiv entrepreneurs; when he advertised the opportunity, three hundred people applied for the twenty-five places on offer. 'These people who will take the course, they will come for four hours to study after they finish their regular job, despite whether there was any shelling that day or not. They will gather in a room which once again has glass in the windows and they will learn, and dream about how they are going to develop their business. And when I am with them, I feel this true spirit of Kharkiv.'

Dima spent time at the Hub in Kupyansk, where most of the customers are military and police because ordinary residents 'have more important problems than coffee' – although he says sometimes people text him to say it actually helps to have somewhere relaxing to go for a few moments, a brief glimpse of that time before the war. 'We will get some drinks there for the summer like espresso tonic, it will be a really cool new menu.' When he asked Sonya, his Kupyansk barista who had been hurt by shrapnel, if she was sure she didn't want to evacuate to somewhere safer, she insisted she wanted to stay; after all, it was her home. Dima says he could understand, because that was Kharkiv's way. 'We have so many damaged buildings, like our coffee shop – in the evening, shelling and rockets, it's all broken, but in the morning hipsters will come and drink cappuccino.' Not for nothing did Kharkiv become known as the 'iron city': 'The people who have stayed here became the basis of the city during war; they were few, but we are united – it is about strength and power. So what would I say about Kharkiv? It is wounded, but not broken.'

Some of the boarded-up windows at Makers were eventually replaced by glass again. On the rest, a local artist painted part of a poem by the writer Maksym Kryvtsov: 'I'll get my life back, I promise.' Kryvtsov, who had joined the army, was killed on the front lines in the winter of 2023. Dima took another trip to Kupyansk to reopen his kiosk there; Sonya the barista had recovered from her injuries and wanted to be back at work. Hamlet Zinkivsky came with him and painted a mural on a destroyed Kupyansk bridge: 'Tired, Concussed, Happy.'

But as 2024 wore on, the rocket and drone attacks became constant, their consequences often devastating. Glide bombs fell with barely any warning, hitting a busy DIY store, a barber shop, city-centre cafes and residential homes. Closer to the border, entire towns were levelled to the ground by Russian bombing: residents were forced to flee their homes in places like Vovchansk, Kozacha Lopan and Staryi Saltiv. Many of them came to Kharkiv, so that homes which had emptied of people fleeing attacks were filled again by those who had been displaced from somewhere even worse.

Kharkiv's streets were scarcely busy any more, even if there were still some families walking through Shevchenko Park on a summer's day, and middle-aged men in swimming trunks taking in the sun in the landscaped park around a wooded area called Sarzhin Yar. At night the city was plunged into complete darkness: no street lights, no traffic lights, and most of the time no GPS either, because it was scrambled during air alarms to frustrate drones. It was all very disorienting.

But there was a city motto, which you could see on billboards everywhere: 'Kharkiv lives and works', as if to reassure people that life would go on. McDonald's had not reopened its branches in Kharkiv, although it had done so in other cities further from the active war zone. But walking past one of their shuttered branches on the central part of Nauky Avenue, my friend noticed lights on in the car park and went to investigate. In the space where McDonald's customers had parked up to enjoy their burgers, there were a bunch of enterprising street food trucks which had set up there instead, selling sushi burgers and bubble tea and ice creams, with light bulbs strung up between the vans and folding chairs for people to sit. On the other side of Freedom Square, the Pakufuda cafe had rigged up a Starlink, to provide some mobile connection while other services were down, and a series of generators, and became busy with customers who could not get lights or internet at home. Snidanishna managed to source a larger generator to keep their kitchen working, and were able to put on outdoor markets at the weekend where people could buy special dishes to eat at tables set up along the pavement terrace. Boris Lomako opened a new bakery, and excitedly showed me the plans for an ambitious project which he wanted to build just outside the city, including a restaurant, shops and a food market with local produce.

The situation in Kupyansk had grown so bad that it was under a mandatory evacuation order, but I went back to Izyum to see Dima Kabanets's new branch of Makers Coffee. His dad Serhii drove me there, while he was dropping off boxes of croissants and cheesecakes and sticky buns, and fresh supplies of coffee. It was a cool and welcoming space which he had managed to put together in just a few days. There were plenty of young customers, queueing up for takeaway flat whites and sharing plates of buns at a couple of outside tables on the pavement. Dima told me that when he had advertised the new jobs there, they were snapped up, in a town where opportunities for young people have been hard to find. On the outside wall of the shop there was a Zinkivsky mural of a chair with some coffee cups. 'Where are you?' it said. 'In reality.' Inside, there was a small exhibition of photographs and text by Maksym Kryvtsov, which he had curated about a month before he was killed in action. The exhibition was all about light: sunlight falling on Donetsk oblast fields, a trench candle, shadows dappling a girl in uniform curled up on a narrow bench. 'Light never ends,' said one of the captions, 'and it begins inside the human heart.' I asked Dima about his plans for the future. Given the situation on the front lines not far away, his answer was tempered by realism. 'Maybe if I can live until tomorrow, that is enough.'

A sign warning of the danger of mines in the destroyed village of Kamyanka.

Top left: Crowd waiting to collect bread from the mobile bakery in the village of Partyzanske, Mykolaiv region.
Top right: Destroyed village, Partyzanske.

Right: Odesa's Pryvoz market.

Top left: Zhenya Mykhailenko with sous chef Vova at his kitchen in Zaporizhzhya.
Top right: Mykyta Virchenko, chef at Tripichya in Kharkiv.

Left: With Oleksii Kolchanov at the Meetty chocolate factory in Kremenchuk.

Left: My favourite *gombovtsi* dish at Snidanishna in Kharkiv.
Right: Lunch dishes at Tripichya.

Right: Maria Timoshenko from Nomer Domu chocolatiers making jam.

Above: Talking to Tamada, deputy commander with the marine brigade.
Right: Tatyana and her husband Kirill with her home-baked sourdough Easter breads.
Below: Dinner in Krynychne, Odesa region, cooked by Tatyana.

Above: Chef inside the Food Train.
Top right: Car waiting for pick up at the Ukrainian Railways Food Train.
Right: Cooks preparing thousands of dishes on the Food Train.

Below: Maria Shpionova, manager of the Food Train, labelling supplies.

Left: Vlad and Yurii on the mobile bakery in Mykolaiv. **Above:** *Syrniki* made at home by Maria Kalenska.

Left: Valerii, known as Maestro, preparing fried potatoes with lard for soldiers at a military hospital in Eastern Ukraine. **Below:** Natalia in her volunteer kitchen.

Above left: Destroyed elementary school in Zorya village, Mykolaiv region.
Above right: Fragment from a burned history book showing Lenin in 1903, amid bomb debris in Kherson.
Right: Inside a destroyed classroom in Zorya village.

Opposite: Baker Yurii, now in the armed forces, at the Khatynka Pekarya in Bucha.

Above: Russian ammunition boxes being repurposed into the roof of a new home in the destroyed village of Kamyanka.
Top right: An elderly woman cooks in a basement without electricity in the frontline town of Siversk.

Bottom right: Yurich's basement in Izyum, where he sheltered sixty-five people during the fighting.
Below: A destroyed building in central Kharkiv.

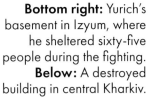

Above: Volunteers in a charity bakery beneath a church in North Saltivka, Kharkiv.

Top Left: Katrya Kalyuzhna, from occupied Kherson region, in the bakery where she works in Lviv.
Left: Lerane Khaybullayeva, from Crimea, in her cafe Crimean Yard in Lviv.
Bottom left: Women unload bread in the frontline city of Lyman.

Top: Outside the mobile bakery at
the Green Theatre space in Odesa.
Bottom left: Mural by LBWS in Odesa
which says 'Mykolaiv is Odesa's shield'.
Bottom right: At the mobile bakery in Odesa.

Opposite: Eggs for sale in
the Novy Rynok, Odesa.

Above: Fancy *syrniki* at the Bakehouse cafe in Kyiv.
Right: Cherries cooking over fire at Igor Mezencev's Forest Dinner near Kyiv.
Below: Staff with mental disabilities making bread at the Good Bread bakery in Kyiv.

Top left: Kostya Tovstakoriy on the bench outside his coffee shop in Odesa.
Top right: Hospitality from a local family in Bessarabia, Odesa region.
Left: Grad rocket in the asphalt, Donetsk region.
Below: Volunteers from Antytila on the road to Kostyantinivka, delivering supplies through Donetsk region.

Memorabilia at Natalia's volunteer canteen, near Pavlohrad, Dnipropetrovsk region.

Chapter Eleven
KHERSON UNDER SIEGE

So much of Ukraine has been laid waste by Russia's war. Cities, towns, villages have been razed to the ground, polluted by mines, hollowed out and slowly destroyed. In Kherson, which has been through the terror of Russian occupation, the heady joy of liberation and now the relentless misery and terror of living just a couple of miles from Russian lines, it has become steadily harder for the dwindling population to carry on.

Many of Kherson's young people left when they could, like Kostya Tovstakoriy, who now runs a coffee shop in a narrow cobbled lane just off one of the main streets in central Odesa, 120 miles to the west. Outside there is a solid-looking black wooden bench, which on closer inspection has a few deep scratches and scuff marks. It's a bench that survived a HIMARS missile attack in occupied Kherson, at Kostya's city-centre cafe where Russian occupiers had set up a position directly opposite. All the windows and the door to his shop were blown out, but the bench was left standing. And so, when he finally relocated to Odesa, he brought it with him.

Before the big war, Kostya had built up a highly regarded coffee business in Kherson, opening I Love Coffee in 2016, one of the first third-wave places in the city. Two years later he opened another branch, then a third. They featured in all the major coffee guides, while customers enjoyed sitting on the bench outside, often posting photographs on social media showing older couples leaning into each other, young girls clutching their takeaway cups, smiling into the sun. But then came the day at the end of February 2022 when everything changed, when Russian tanks and troops stormed into the city, and life would never be the same again. Kostya closed his shops, because there was no business selling coffee during occupation, and spent his days keeping his head down, dodging through back streets if he had to go outside. 'I moved like this in the city, hiding from the Russians, because you never knew what they were going to do.' He and his family managed to escape, spending twelve hours on the road to drive the forty miles to Ukrainian-held territory and the city of Mykolaiv, and eventually onwards to start life again in Odesa.

Liberation came to Kherson in November 2022, when Ukrainian forces managed to recapture a huge portion of territory along the right bank of the Dnipro river. There were heady scenes of jubilation as Ukrainian soldiers entered the city, joyfully embraced by residents who rushed out to greet them with flowers and flags that they'd been forced to hide away for months. But the euphoria was short-lived: the Russians dug into well-fortified positions across the river and began relentlessly shelling Kherson and surrounding villages, hitting buses and shops and cultural centres and schools. In the summer of 2023, large parts of the city were flooded after Russia bombed the Nova Kakhovka dam, sending torrents of water gushing through villages and city streets, ruining everything in their path. Kostya's shops were in the middle of a danger zone, but remarkably he managed to keep one of them open, with two employees who wanted to carry on working. 'I don't make any money, it's my own money which I use to keep them working, but my baristas have jobs.' And in a city where regular work and a secure income are ever scarcer, that has become a vital lifeline.

I had made a rapid car journey into Kherson in 2023, delivering aid supplies a few weeks after the floods. But I took a longer trip the following spring, to visit Kostya's I Love Coffee shop in the city, as well as some other food businesses which had somehow managed to keep going. With us was the American journalist Zarina Zabrisky, who had spent months living in the city under constant bombardment, making a documentary about life under this unbearable siege. 'We will meet in the place which has the best *syrniki* in Kherson,' she promised, and so we arrived at the pretty-looking Cafe Verona first thing in the morning to meet the owner Maksym, a young man with tiredness etched into his face, who had somehow managed to hold things together over these impossibly difficult months. It was a bright sunny day, shimmering with the first warmth of spring, but on the drive in, the city had been almost deserted, although there were some local council workers cutting the grass verge by the side of the road. It seemed unwise to linger outside on the terrace, even wearing body armour, so we hurried inside. Maksym came over to our table, looking exhausted. 'It is the most difficult time of all our twelve years in business,' he said. 'We have no customers, no visitors, the city is almost empty and we are located in the centre, which is a very dangerous area. The Russians are maybe five kilometres from here, on the other side of the river. And they are shooting bombs almost every day, every night. In the morning I wake up and come to work, and I don't know what condition I will find the place in.' Cups of strong coffee arrived, while Maksym explained that the restaurant had not made a single penny in profit for almost two years, bringing in just about enough to cover the wages of his few remaining members of staff.

When he and his mother had opened Cafe Verona, they wanted to create an upmarket restaurant which would stand out from the myriad 'sushi-pizza' places which had sprung up across Kherson. They invested in fancy equipment, experimented with new cooking techniques and paid their chef top rates. 'He earned what he would make in a top Kyiv restaurant. There must have been about a hundred places in the downtown area alone, but we were in the top five in the whole region.' They served around three to four hundred customers a day: 'We were full from opening to closing time, it never stopped.' He had sold his flat to buy the property and everything they made was ploughed back into improvements: putting in some oak furniture, and installing any noisy equipment in the basement to cause minimal disruption to their neighbours. Ironically, this proved a godsend during the occupation, when they had several hundred litres of both unfiltered and drinking water held in reserve, as well as 200 kilos of coffee which they had only just bought. 'We managed to share our water with other people, because after the Russians came there was nothing. And our store of groceries was enough for my family to survive for half a year, as we refused to buy any Russian products.'

Maksym kept the restaurant open throughout those traumatic months, because he was worried that if it closed, Russians or local collaborators would break in and smash the place up. 'If we didn't create the impression that we are working, they might rob our cafe and work without us.' He managed to make bread for the Red Cross for a few months, using flour donated by friends. 'We tied white material to the car which made deliveries, because it could be shot at.' He described how they had done their best not to serve any

Russians who came in. 'We could tell, because of their accent. So if they asked "Can we take a seat?" we would say no, we have no chefs, we have no food. We can only do coffee to go. And then we would make a really bad coffee, and charge twice the usual price, so for that Russian it's both terrible and very expensive. Next time he won't come back.'

When liberation finally came, Maksym powered up the coffee machine to full capacity and began handing out free drinks to people celebrating in the central square. But life was extremely hard. 'We had no lights, no mobile phone connection, no water – the Russians had poured liquid concrete into the wells, which meant none of the city had water. We had a generator which was just about enough to keep the coffee machine switched on.' He was glad he had the cafe, he said: 'It helped me to survive. I don't know how other people survived. But if we saw residents coming back, and thought our nightmare had finished, in reality it had only just started.' Exhausted by the constant shelling, people started leaving the city again for safety elsewhere. Maksym hung on to one team of staff, and managed to keep Verona open from nine till four in the afternoon, then extended the closing time a little until six. He had just paid off the loan on his house, which his family had built themselves, and his car was on credit. 'But I have no money to pay this credit. Sometimes it is like a worm, eating me up, this worry. Sometimes I think before I get thrown out of my house, out of my business, maybe I should go to another city and look for jobs. But for example, if I went to Odesa, I would have to pay rent for my room, to pay for my goods, to eat somewhere. And it's really expensive there. A coffee in Odesa is as much as a hundred hyrvnias [just over £2], whereas here it will cost thirty.' There was no government help for businesses, he said; they were expected to pay their own way.

So he stayed put, with his family, and his son who was born under occupation, whose short life had known only war. While the restaurant, with its grand coffee machine and pared-back menu, 'helps me to survive under the missiles.' The *syrniki* arrived, a large portion split onto two plates – one for me and the other for my Odesa journalist and fixer colleague, Artem. It was served simply with a small dish of sour cream. Maksym scrolled through his phone for photos showing what the restaurant had been like before the war, and its glamorous-looking food. He paused on a picture of the *syrniki*, which they used to serve with a mound of fresh berries and fruit coulis. 'It's much too expensive to buy that nowadays. So this is how it comes today, very plain.' They were still delicious, crisp around the edges and not too sweet. While we ate, he found another video, which started with a scene of the outdoor terrace, calm and quiet and getting ready for service, and suddenly switched to some CCTV: a bomb explodes, right outside, glass and debris flying everywhere. The camera pans hectically along the pavement; there is the ugly crunching sound of boots on broken glass. The sign on the door which once said '09:00 to 22:00' is crossed out, replaced by '16:00'. But despite it all, Cafe Verona has remained open; as we left a couple of customers were walking in, coffees were on order, and they are just about holding on, in the hope of better times to come.

Just under a mile away was a pub, Kot Patriot, with a British-style red telephone box in the main bar, which had been converted into a dessert cabinet full of tempting-looking cakes. Downstairs, in the relative safety of the basement, there was a restaurant, where I had been told they served a very decent borsch. We scanned the lengthy menu: there was even a choice between borsch with meat and a vegan version, which came with spring onion and garlic on the side, and some freshly made flatbread. Dmytro, the barman and waiter, brought it over and began telling stories about life under occupation, describing how he had been faced with drunk and rude Russian customers, who several times had threatened him at gunpoint, trying to get served after hours. Things had been much quieter since they left, he insisted, while persuading me and Artem to order a second plate of *deruny*, fried-potato pancakes stuffed with mushrooms. 'Now it's more or less normal, except of course there are sometimes explosions outside, which can be scary. My daughter stays in Kyiv because she's afraid to come back.'

We struggled back into our body armour to go outside again, and drove through deserted streets to the city's remaining branch of I Love Coffee. There was a familiar-looking bench outside, exactly like the one Kostya had brought to Odesa, although no one was sitting outside in the afternoon sun. 'That's the river,' Artem said, pointing down the slope. You could see it, the water gleaming on the horizon. 'Three kilometres to Russians.' We turned swiftly into the coffee shop, where the front window was protected by a large pile of sandbags. The barista, Nastya, made a couple of spectacular cups of Americano, which cost around half the price you'd pay in Odesa, and came over to chat. She had been working there for a year and a half when the full-scale invasion happened, and had no work at all while it was closed. Now she said, she was more than happy to be back at her job. 'I don't need any extra motivation to be here: I love my work and I know my customers. Maybe sometimes I don't want to have to wake up early but most of the time I enjoy it. We have our regular clients: during the occupation a small community supported us because they hated the Russians, and now new people come here too.'

Business was quiet on a Sunday afternoon and we only saw a few other customers, but Nastya said it got busier during the week, when people came by in the mornings on the way to work, or during their break. 'This place is a part of life; you can come for a meeting or just to sit on the bench and have some sunshine. For our customers it is a reason to go outside, to take a walk and have somewhere else to go.' Not many people wander out and about in Kherson, given the constant risks of shelling, but Nastya insisted she still felt perfectly comfortable there, going to work and looking after her cats. Her parents had moved to a safer part of the country in the west, she said, so she didn't have to worry about them. 'Recently I went to visit them, but it was not easy for me, because it was a big, busy city full of people and I found it much too noisy. So really I like to work in my own city; we are used to things here, it is our home.'

Back in the city centre we had arranged another meeting in the cafe of the main Silpo supermarket. The outside was almost completely hidden behind the ubiquitous plywood boards, with a large concrete bomb shelter near the front door. Inside, it was a completely different story: beautifully laid out displays of fresh produce, a large bakery counter, many kinds of fish and meat. When the Russians had occupied Kherson, they took over the Silpo and renamed it 'Sytny Market', stocking it with goods from Belarus and occupied Crimea. Local residents said everything was far inferior to the Ukrainian products they were used to, as well as costing a lot more, while Russian forces had also looted the place – stealing items as random as a fish smokehouse, self-checkout machines and electronic scales. After liberation, the Silpo management was determined to reopen the Kherson store as soon as possible, restoring the looted equipment and starting with a limited range of goods. Once they managed to resume deliveries, they filled the shelves again with Ukrainian produce and brands. Pride in local food was another example of Ukraine's determination to reassert its cultural identity, which had been subsumed for so long by Russian and Soviet imperialism.

At the in-store cafe, we sat down with local food shop owner and volunteer Olha, who lost her fiancé and a close friend when they were hit by a Russian mine in the summer of 2023. She had managed to keep her shop open during the long months of occupation, even though it was a struggle to get both customers and supplies. Sometimes, she said, she would find out that her products were being resold on the black market. She was especially angry about the terrible standard of groceries which the occupied supermarkets began selling. 'They were really, really bad quality and a really, really high price. They started bringing things from Crimea and then collaborators got contracts with companies in [occupied] Donetsk, and brought their groceries here. One guy, who became a regional minister under the Russian administration, set up an alcohol and cigarette business. He went to the market in the absolute worst street and traded the vodka and cigarettes himself. After the occupation they published a list of collaborators and I thought, I know this guy – not because he is a minister but because I bought cigarettes from him down at the market. And not even by the packet – he would sell single ones!'

The food shop had been in Olha's family for twenty years, but the war brought near-impossible challenges. After the Nova Kakhovka dam was blown up, her shop was in one of the areas that got flooded. 'We survived the flood, even though the water reached around one metre forty centimetres high; a lot of our equipment got damaged, but we managed to fix it and dry it out. We've been hit by shelling several times, but we are still working. Our power gets cut off; after a hit, sometimes we don't have electricity for two weeks, but we are still working.' She somehow found the energy to take on more humanitarian work, partnering with World Central Kitchen to deliver hot meals to people: 'Because of the shelling they just deliver everything to our location, then we take it to everyone on the list. And because a lot of people don't have power, they come to us to charge their phones. We can offer some stability to them because we are open every day, without a day off. Sometimes they just come here because otherwise they wouldn't have a chance to see another person.' She was also frustrated by dealing with red tape and bureaucracy, combined with the lack of government help for small businesses, which were expected to manage on their own. 'The last time the shelling hit us, customers started asking straight away when we would start working again. It was maybe two hours after that attack that we reopened, which was stressful, yes.'

Olha showed me some photographs of colourful desserts which she had started making out of jelly spiked with vodka, with designs which looked like gently blooming flowers. 'It is spring, and after the floods, after the shelling, people go out and start planting flowers in their gardens. You can't go for a walk or a drive along the river in this place because the Russians are right across the other side. But we are still able to sit in this Silpo, in a comfortable cafe, listening to music, because of the work of our army and our defenders.' She got up to go, saying she had friends coming over in the evening, and vodka jelly cakes to prepare. On the way to the door, she turned to smile: 'Everything will be good,' she said.

A few months after that visit, there was a new nightmare for the residents who remained in Kherson. My journalist friend Zarina Zabrisky was one of the few reporters still there, doggedly recording every time the Russians sent up their small FPV drones to chase civilians, before dropping grenades on them. It happened dozens of times every week, hitting people on buses, on bicycles, in the gardens of their homes. It became almost impossible even to venture outside, with posters all over town organised by Olha, informing people to run for shelter immediately if they heard a drone flying over their heads. Kherson's streets had already been almost deserted; this new threat turned the place into a ghost town. And in the winter, without the cover of leaves on the trees, it would become even worse. I thought of Olha and her shop near the river, who'd had two of her work cars damaged by drones, the coffee shop flanked by sandbags, Maksym in his restaurant, which was newly scarred by shrapnel. Somehow they were hanging on, Zarina told me, through this overwhelming cruelty of Russia's war.

Chapter Twelve

THIS LAND IS OUR LAND

The gently rolling hills around Kamyanka, with their pastures, their fruit orchards and lush meadows, were once rich in crops. The fertile soil was perfect for growing wheat, rapeseed, sunflower and corn, but the war has reduced it to a wasteland.

The small village, which lies on the main road running from Izyum in the north-eastern Kharkiv region, due east towards the border with Donetsk region, has been completely destroyed. It is a shocking sight as you drive over the hill and see the wreckage of houses spread out across the valley on both sides of the road. There is nothing left of people's homes, their farms, their dreams. But among the piles of rubble, you can also see a few of the distinctive blue tarpaulins erected by aid agencies, where people are starting to return. You have to watch where you are treading, because everywhere are red signs warning of the danger of mines. Some of them have been replaced by white rags tied to fence posts, which show that the area has been cleared.

Terrible war crimes happened in Kamyanka, when it was under occupation during those grim months in 2022. Eighteen months after it was liberated, the Russians are still only a few dozen miles away, but there are residents who want to live there again, and there are organisations to help them.

A Swiss demining charity called FSD has spent many months working in the area, while a local NGO called Unity and Strength has been helping people to rebuild their shattered properties. One of their volunteers, Marcin, agreed to take me there, to meet some farmers who were determined to get back to their land.

On the way in, we drove past a large notice which local people had put up by the side of the road: 'Please! Help us rebuild the village!' it says, with a link to a QR code and some bank details. In the driveway beside what was once Valerii Vertsun's farm, a huge concrete slab has been dragged in front of a turning, next to a destroyed house. 'Warning!' is painted across it in big red letters. 'Do not proceed any further, there are mines.' We follow Valerii into the yard: I know it has been checked carefully for ordnance, but given the big concrete warning sign I walk carefully on the asphalt, remembering the hostile environment advice: 'Follow exactly the person in front.' Much of his farm was destroyed in the early days of the full-scale war when a guided air bomb hit his garage, where he'd been storing several hundred cubic metres of fuel. He left with his family for nearby Izyum, but that town was coming under increasing attack. His wife and children went to western Ukraine, and then to the centre of the country and Dnipro, because it was simply unaffordable to stay where they were. 'Uzhhorod was more expensive than Paris!' he says. Valerii had wanted to stay near the farm but after a shell hit the house where he was staying, he drove to another small town a bit further away. As the Russian occupiers advanced even closer, he realised he would have to leave the area altogether and joined his family in Dnipro, leaving everything behind.

We walk through the ruined farmyard, surrounded by piles of twisted metal and burned-out farm vehicles. 'In that last warehouse, the Russians were keeping their Grad missiles,' he says. Most of the place had been levelled in those first weeks, but there was part of a roof left on one barn, so the Russians had used it as their storage place. 'During the counteroffensive the Ukrainians hit it with a HIMARS missile, everything exploded and the whole lot burned down.' The explosion was so huge that pieces of the warehouse were scattered hundreds of metres away. Somehow, two truckloads of Grads and a Kamaz lorry full of other weapons were untouched, and the advancing Ukrainian forces seized the chance to redeploy them. 'You might call it lend-lease. Recycling. Return to the original owner.' There were intense battles for control of the area. 'About fifteen kilometres away there's a town called Dolyna – our army was holding it and the Russians tried hard to get there. One of the nearby villages was going from one hand to the other, all the time.' Those months of heavy fighting left everything in ruins. 'Fifteen hundred tonnes of wheat burned down here. There were eight hundred tonnes of sunflower, and six hundred tonnes of corn. It all burned.' The expensive American tractors and combine harvesters went up in flames too.

Valerii only found out the extent of the damage when he managed to get back, after the liberation of Izyum in September 2022. Ukrainian soldiers hoisted the blue and yellow flag above the wrecked administration building in the town's main square and Valerii drove there, hoping to get to the farm. 'We weren't allowed there immediately as the roads had not been cleared; the sappers went around with their markers where the mines were, and that was basically all the roads.' Finally he was allowed to see his property. 'All the territory was still covered in butterfly mines, so I entered very carefully, looked around, cried a bit, and that was it, I had to leave again.' Some of the big wooden boxes which had contained the Russian Grad missiles were still lying around. 'I sat on one of those boxes and said to myself, I can't get too emotional. My job is to start rebuilding, and if I get too emotional, I will just break down.' He told himself it was nothing he hadn't done before. 'I'd had the farm for eighteen years, there was nothing here before I came, just a couple of buildings, and the rest I built myself.'

In front of the destroyed barn, we could see what was left of his tractors, planting and combine machines. There are two John Deere machines which cost a quarter of a million dollars apiece. He says he's managed to pillage the most badly damaged ones for spare parts, while two of the tractors are being repaired in Izyum, but he's been waiting in vain for some kind of compensation to help fix the rest. 'I hired someone from an institute in Kharkiv to document exactly what was lost. If only I had the means to rebuild it all, I could fix everything in one summer. I built it myself in the first place, so I know exactly what needs to be done and how much work it will take.'

His biggest challenge is the countless mines which the Russians threw everywhere, from the large anti-tank mines which would destroy a tractor to the coloured plastic ones known as butterfly mines, which could seriously maim anyone who trod on one or tried to pick it up. The FSD charity has been doing its best, but it is frustratingly slow work. First they used drones to map the fields and work out where everything was. 'They started the technical work here last September, although they decided to clear the other side of the village first. They bought a machine to dig up the bigger mines, but it isn't 100 per cent accurate, so they have to go back through again with a hand-held detector.' The sappers had to stop work during the winter months because the ground was too hard, and the snow made it impossible to see anything. 'To demine the whole of Kamyanka and surrounding fields will probably take decades,' he said, staring into the horizon. 'If they had more equipment, it might be faster.' Marcin steps in to explain more. 'They bought one machine made by the KhTZ tractor factory in Kharkiv, which is so big that a whole district of the city is named after it. It shows that they're focusing on this demining technology and giving a boost to the local economy at the same time.'

Valerii said he saw the investment in demining as a sign that the Ukrainian government was truly committed to holding on to the territory. We were speaking a week or so before the renewed Russian offensive in the Kharkiv region, and the intensive bombing around Vovchansk and other border towns. There was a lot of controversy about how far the Ukrainians had dug in and prepared proper defences, with questions around whether it was all happening too hastily and too late. The Russians had sacrificed hundreds of thousands of men to make their creeping advances, but in the areas which they had seized, they were known for ruthlessly fortifying their own defensive lines.

Driving through Kharkiv region in late April 2024, you could see deep trenches and observation points snaking through the fields, with long lines of anti-tank barricades. 'They are building more trenches now along the Oskil river,' Valerii said. 'I don't know if they will use them or not, but the fact that they are building them is a sign of political will: if the Russians try to get closer again, they are not going to let them cross here.' He was staying optimistic about the future, and the chances of getting back to his land again. 'I hope that in the autumn we can start planting wheat, then we can harvest that and make a bit of money, then we can use that to fix the next thing. Step by step.' His dealer told him it would cost a hundred thousand Euros to mend his truck. 'I won't let any of those Kamaz trucks on my property again, because they are Russian.' He once had thirty-two employees and has been trying to keep on the people who worked for him before the war; they have been helping to fix up the machines and providing some security. They would work the land again, he said, when it was all ready.

The wind is picking up: there is a sharp chill to the air. Beside the tangled remains of the grain warehouses, there are still some of the olive-green Grad missile boxes, stacked anyhow amid the wreckage. 'I built this farm once,' Valerii says. 'Perhaps that was just training and now I can build it for real. People are always saying, "Oh, I made so many mistakes the first time, I would do it differently if I had a second chance." But this, I really did get it right the first time. I spent so much time planning and thinking about it, and I will rebuild it exactly as it was.' It would be easy to be overcome by despair, standing here in such a devastated landscape, but Valerii is looking to the future. 'They will bring all this back. No one will let this soil just sit here, because it is true Ukrainian soil, famous for its fertility. Ukraine will become a regular European country, and everything will be fine.'

These were such optimistic words, but they seemed in complete contrast to the ruined buildings we were driving past as we crossed the main road into the rest of the village. Some of them are still defaced by graffiti scrawled by the Russian occupiers in spray paint, giant letters Z and V, the letters which Moscow's forces used to identify their military vehicles during the full-scale invasion. The deminers have pinned up a few rows of white rags, and a handful of residents are returning, to start the formidable job of restoring their homes. On the corner of one street, we pull over at a place which Unity and Strength is helping to rebuild. Next to a new breeze-block wall, there is a pile of Russian ammunition boxes which they are planning to break up into wooden planks, to build a storeroom for sunflower seeds. On the other side of the path is a small memorial: a photograph of a Ukrainian soldier fixed to a telegraph pole, and some blue and yellow ribbons and flowers. Marcin tells me he was a man from the 95th Brigade who had been killed during the bitter fighting in 2022. 'The occupiers would not let anyone bury him, it happened only after the village was liberated. Now his colleagues come to leave flowers for him.' Marcin shouts over the breeze blocks to see if anyone is home: we are looking for another farmer, Vova Korniicha and his wife Lyuda. They are not back yet from a trip to buy supplies in Kharkiv. Instead their mother-in-law is planting tulips in the garden of the half-built home, 'so that there will be something beautiful to look at, out of the new windows!' She calls Vova, and we arrange to meet at a roadside coffee stand near Izyum.

The young couple had returned to the village soon after de-occupation to find that only a single wall of their home was left standing. At that point, there was no outside help. Vova was so impatient to get back to his land that he tried pulling out some of the mines with his bare hands, using a shovel and some secateurs. They had built up their business for more than twenty years, ever since the old kolkhoz collective farm system set up under the Soviet Union was disbanded and they were allowed to own some land. Even then, he described the long and complicated struggle against bureaucracy and vested interests to secure the fields which they had been working on for years. 'At the beginning, I was working the land myself. Then I hired my brother, then my wife's brother, so it was a real family business. When there was a lot of physical work to do, we would get in some extra help. And that's how we lived until 2022.' As well as the staple crops – sunflower, wheat and corn – they had set aside some of the land for experiments. 'We started growing some vegetables, peas and sweetcorn, tomatoes and cucumbers and watermelon. I had a friend who would give me lots of advice. We had a go at growing sugar beet, but it was a bit too challenging. That was an experiment which didn't quite come off, but we certainly tried a bit of everything!'

We are sitting in one of the branches of Kulynychi, a bakery chain popular with soldiers. Across the road, a tank has parked up and some young men are climbing out of the hatch to fetch coffees and shawarma. We order some paper cups of tea. 'We had everything we needed, except our own combine, but we were completely independent and finally able to plan five years ahead,' Vova says, although they were faced with their fair share of challenges. 'We had borrowed some storage space in a friend's warehouse in Sloviansk to keep our sunflower seeds. But in 2014 the whole lot burned down in the fighting.' When he got together with his wife Lyuda, they had planted some peas. 'I told her, when we sell these peas, we'll be able to buy a house in Izyum. But we've never been able to harvest them. The war just flipped our whole world upside down.'

The couple had both been living in Kamyanka before they got married, and Vova jokes that he only moved in with Lyuda because he had grown up with four brothers and sisters, while she had a much smaller family. 'You just found a place where they liked you,' Lyuda says. Her parents used to help out around the farm, but getting back to work on their devastated land will be a formidable task. Before the war, they had around 120 hectares. When they were finally able to come back and inspect it, they found out that 90 per cent of it was mined. 'I managed to clean up about 28 hectares myself,'

Vova says, adding that he is grateful to friends who provided some technical assistance. But it will be a long time before it is completely safe. 'Just yesterday, some military guys came and found some munitions with explosives which were right on the edge of one of my fields. And that's a year and a half after it was de-occupied. I knew something was left there so I had been avoiding the area. And the mines which I pulled out myself are still lying around somewhere.' But at least some help is trickling through. 'It is really hard. You have to try working the fields so that the soil doesn't deteriorate. We have plenty of motivation, but we just need the tools.' The UN Food and Agriculture Organisation gave him some grain to plant. 'It's very limited, just one type of grain. Another organisation said they could provide eight types of seeds, but they haven't actually brought anything yet. We got given a voucher, but it's only valid for a few weeks and we're worried that it will run out before anything is available.'

They aren't used to asking for help. 'If everything was normal we could manage everything ourselves, but the price of everything has gone down and the dollar went up, so effectively that means sunflower is worth less than half of what it was before the war. But we are really thankful to groups like the FAO and the Swiss deminers for what they are doing. We just want to get back to our land.'

His hands are deeply ingrained with decades of working that black, fertile soil, and I think of all the life which they literally ploughed into their land. The hated Russian ammunition boxes, which will be turned into a storage space for new crops. And his mother-in-law, busy planting tulips, bringing a bright patch of beauty to a place visited by so much trauma and death.

In the nearby village of Studenok, residents have been able to start working their land, growing fruit and vegetables in the fields behind their homes. A Kharkiv charity called Volonterska decided to help them find a market for their produce, and created a new project, the 'De-occupation Shop'. They'd been active in the region, helping civilians from the moment the February 2022 invasion was launched. Meriam Yol, one of the founders of the project, explained that they had been helping with rebuilding work for small farms which had been destroyed during the fighting. And once the energy blackouts started up again, they began providing generators too.

But they wanted to do more, and their team went to some of the villages to ask people there what they needed to help them make a decent living, and become financially independent again. In August 2023 they had been helping with reconstruction work in a village called Dovhenke. 'As we were heading out, a lady called Lyuda, who was one of the people we'd been helping, gave us some corn which she had grown herself in her garden. We tried the corn, and it was delicious. It made us think – wow, other people really need to try it.' They brought more of Lyuda's corn back to Kharkiv and partnered with ten cafes and restaurants in the city, who either sold the corn fresh or cooked a special dish with it. 'Some made ice cream, some baked it or cooked various things with it – it was super fast and impromptu. Lyuda was able to earn more than 20,000 hyrvnias (around £500) without having to do much. Well of course she had demined the garden and grew the corn herself, but she didn't have to worry about the logistics or sales. She just handed the corn to us, we sold it and gave her the money.'

The Volonterska team met up with Dmytro Nazarchuk, one of the owners of a street food space in central Kharkiv called 7 Warehouses. It's a cool and modern site, with a mezzanine level where people can sit and eat, and various street food stalls underneath. There's a landscaped garden in the middle, with beautifully designed wooden chairs and tables. 'Dmytro wouldn't leave me alone for weeks, saying Meri, come on, let's do something.' He offered the De-occupation Shop a site in the venue for free. 'I said we need to turn it from something impromptu into a product with a concept.' The team spent six months working out how to make the project work, from the logistics to the legal framework. 'Whom should we sell to, why should people buy it, how would the farmers grow it and so on.' Then they began working on the funding and development issues, and finally chose six farmers to begin working with, all from Studenok. 'They already have the greenhouses, we gave them the seeds, the fertilisers and equipment. They are all fully on board and involved.'

The charity had always set out to give people the means to help themselves. 'In the spring of 2023, Volonterska provided seeds to more than 6,000 farmsteads. We give them something they can grow rather than just bags of dried pasta. It has a positive psychological effect, and people keep busy. This year we've done the same with 15,000 small farms. We just have to keep adapting every day to the conditions around us. The other week a missile struck the warehouse of one of our suppliers.' The entire order for the De-occupation Shop had been waiting in a Nova Poshta storage site in Kharkiv, which was destroyed in a missile strike. 'We had motor cultivators, rakes, shovels in that order. Fortunately there were no greenhouses, because losing those would have been even worse.' Their contractor refunded the money they had lost, and although the pop-up shop opening had to be delayed, it stayed on track for the summer.

'We will start by selling lots of vegetables: cucumbers, courgettes, tomatoes, radishes, garlic and herbs, and one of our farmers is trying some sweet potatoes. There will be apples and apricots from a neighbouring village, but they will come later. As things grow, we will start selling them.'

I managed to visit the pop-up shop in late summer, just days after a huge forest fire had swept through parts of the region they had been helping. Hundreds of houses in Studenok were damaged, almost half of the village. Maria, the young girl who was manning the till, told me that the small farmers they worked with had somehow managed to save the bulk of their land from the flames. 'We are saying that this is a miracle,' she said. There were crates of salad vegetables for sale, heritage tomatoes and small knobbly cucumbers, potatoes and courgettes. I bought a bag of tomatoes, and was persuaded into some jars of local honey and cherry jam, along with some salt they had flavoured with green herbs. They were also running an emergency fundraiser, to help the villagers who had been impacted by the fire. 'I am so glad to work here,' Maria said. 'It feels like something important.'

The villagers they work with have been living through an incredibly traumatic ordeal, first under occupation, then fleeing their homes and facing the challenge of repairing huge amounts of damage to start life and business all over again. Meriam says the De-occupation Shop is designed to give them exactly the right kind of help. 'It's a way for them to earn income, without worrying about logistics. For example, they used to sell their produce in Izyum or Kramatorsk, not in Kharkiv. But there are very few people now living in those places. So, practically speaking, this shop provides money for them.' The equipment which the charity provided, including greenhouses, is also there to stay. But beyond that there is the psychological support of knowing that someone has their back. 'Every time we visit to pick up vegetables, which is at least twice a week, they are happy, they are doing work, they tell us that seedlings have sprouted, that they're replanting things.' It also has a positive impact for people in Kharkiv, she says, a city reeling under the impact of each new Russian offensive, with constant bomb attacks and air alerts lasting as long as twenty hours. 'If everyone closed and nobody did anything new, it would be a miserable state of affairs.'

Chapter Thirteen

THE WORLD'S FIRST FOOD TRAIN

I have a special bond with Ukrainian trains. I've travelled thousands of miles in their sleeper compartments, shuttling across the country night after night, once even taking a 700-mile round trip from Odesa and back, to visit someone in Kharkiv for lunch. My obsession began with the former Ukrainian Railways boss Oleksandr Kamyshin, who became a familiar presence on social media with his defiant slogan 'Keep Running'. Throughout 2022, he would frequently post about their near 100 per cent punctuality record, even when track or infrastructure was bombed. He set up evacuation trains to carry tens of thousands of people to safer cities in the west, while freight services took food aid and medical supplies the other way. Railway stations were swiftly turned into 'invincibility hubs', providing people with shelter, mobile phone connections and a place to get hot tea and some warmth. The railway company began working closely with humanitarian groups like World Central Kitchen, and the philanthropist Howard Buffett, son of the US billionaire Warren Buffett. And in the spirit of 'everything is possible', they came up with the idea of a Food Train, a dedicated mobile kitchen which would be able to travel to the areas most in need of help and provide thousands of hot meals every day.

With funding from the Howard Buffett Foundation, a small team of designers and engineers at a repair depot in the Chernihiv region finally managed to make it a reality, transforming six carriages into the world's first self-contained kitchen train, which was ready to go into use by autumn 2023. The whole thing was a triumph of creativity and engineering: at one end was a carriage with a tank filled with 27,000 litres of water, complete with filtration and a pump system. Next was the accommodation for the twenty or so people who would work on board for two weeks at a time, sleeping on bunks in the regular four-berth night train sleeper compartments, only one at each end had been refitted with a shower and washing machine. Then came a carriage fitted out as a cold kitchen, where salads and other dishes which didn't need cooking would be prepared, and meals packed into their containers. Next a hot kitchen featuring four large combi steam ovens, each capable of cooking a thousand portions at a time, and a pot-wash section. There was a carriage containing a fridge, freezer and space for dry goods, and in the final one at the back, two generators with a total capacity of 400kw.

After weeks of trying, I finally managed to arrange a meeting with the railway team in Kyiv, including project manager Artur Botchenko, who'd just returned from a long stint working on board as it travelled throughout the Kharkiv region. With that black humour which Ukrainians have become famous for, some of the staff called it the Doomsday Train, because wherever something bad was happening, it was ready to go. I explained all about my Ukrainian Railways obsession and how much I had enjoyed my many long trips on the night trains. Except perhaps the one time I was going to Dnipro, and everything had sold out except the third-class communal sleeper carriage known as Platskart, where everyone sleeps on rows of narrow, shelf-type bunks, feet dangling over the edge because the beds are about six inches too short. 'Oh, so you went Platskart...' Oleksander the press officer asked, trying to suppress a laugh. 'And which seat did you book?' I had to admit I had been completely ignorant of the layout when I bought the ticket. 'The one on the far edge by the door.' This time they all burst out laughing. 'That's the worst place in the entire carriage! As I'm sure you realised! And by the way, don't take this Platskart in the summer. No air conditioning. We call it the hot box.'

By now we had bonded over my misfortune, but arranging to join them on the Food Train was understandably tricky. 'The whole point of this train is to come as close as possible to the front line, the front cities which don't have an electricity supply. So we don't disclose the exact location, or the whereabouts of the train,' Artur explained. 'For safety reasons we can't reveal the details of where and how the food will be distributed. Although it's not like we can hide a six-car-long train completely out of sight.'

From the outset, the Food Train team had built up a network with charities and hospitals in the east and south of Ukraine that would be most in need of help. 'We have spreadsheets, and we constantly communicate with these social organisations and volunteers. It is the first train of its kind in the world, so everything is a new experience; we are doing it all for the first time.' Along with eight railway workers, they had around twelve kitchen workers on each two-week rotation. 'All of them have been volunteering before this; sometimes they worked at the stations, or with World Central Kitchen, we make the most of the resources we have. We have got just the number of people we need to get the work done.'

After assuring them that I wouldn't be posting anything online which might give away the location, they agreed I could visit when the train had arrived in Kharkiv. 'The staff usually start at 3 a.m. or even earlier,' Oleksander warned. 'You'll have to be at the station before five, then the station manager will meet you and take you on board.'

A couple of days later, I turned up at Kharkiv's main train station at dawn along with my local journalist friend and interpreter Yevhen. We were led through a deserted tunnel to the furthest platform of all, where we could see a long train emblazoned with brightly coloured graphics, and the words 'Poizd Kukhnya', or Food Train in Ukrainian. It was even more impressive in real life, and already buzzing with activity. Maria, the train manager, an energetic young woman who showed no traces of tiredness despite having been up for several hours, conjured up some coffee and started to show us around. 'We will be delivering ten and a half thousand portions today,' she explained. 'There's a new menu every day, all the side dishes and the salads change. When it's ready we pack everything into thermal boxes with the name of the receiver on the side. Then the train will be moving. It will be refilled with supplies for the next day. But now, we are preparing *kotlety* – a patty made of chicken mince, with pearl barley and cabbage.'

Even at such an unearthly hour, the energy on board was palpable, with loud pop music playing throughout the carriage as the mostly young people in the team set about assembling the meals into individual containers. Maria ushered us forward. 'This is where we keep the dried mixes for the soups, which get mixed with boiling water. Often it will be borsch, sometimes mushroom or bean soup.' In the hot kitchen area, a chef was busy loading trays into one of the shiny new combi ovens, stepping deftly aside as one of the others carried steaming containers past. With so little space to manoeuvre, economy of movement was clearly paramount, although everything had clearly been designed for maximum efficiency.

The kitchen team's schedule sounded relentless, with so much work to get through. 'Sometimes they get up at midnight, sometimes three or four o'clock, work through until eleven or noon, have a break and then start again until six in the evening. Go to bed at seven.' One of the volunteers, a young woman called Olha, said she had been working as a copywriter in Kyiv when the train opportunity came up on a closed chat group shared by her soldier boyfriend, and she seized the chance to help. Next to her, a woman called Larissa said she had taught psychology at a Kyiv university before the full-scale war. But she wanted her grandchildren to grow up in a peaceful Ukraine, and so here she was, on the train, boxing up portions of chicken and salad with lightning efficiency. There were certainly no complaints about the workload.

For several weeks in that spring of 2024, Kharkiv had been coming under ever more frequent attack, making the Food Train's work even more important, especially after the city's primary energy sources had been destroyed. The air raid siren in the city barely stopped going off throughout the day and night. During one of the alarms, as we stood on the tracks, we heard a glide bomb exploding, and Yevhen pointed out a cloud of smoke billowing up behind the treeline. Railway infrastructure had been hit; later it emerged that one Ukrainian Railways employee had been killed, and another was injured. Work on the Food Train, like the rest of the station, carried on.

Large boxes filled with hundreds of portions of food began being stacked up outside the train, while Maria checked numbers against a spreadsheet and wrote the names of the organisations which would be taking them in big letters on the side. There was a tightly organised schedule of vans and cars from various volunteer groups, which had permission to drive right next to the train tracks to pick up their orders. One man had brought along a large black Labrador, which leapt out of his truck and bounded up to the train steps as if he was supervising the entire process.

Yevhen and I drove across town to the city's Third Regional psychiatric hospital, one of the many places the deliveries were destined for. It had just been damaged by a Russian strike and had reached out to the train team to ask for help. The hospital staff were exhausted and nervous, and led us through the grounds to the spot where one of the S-300 missiles had landed in the early hours of the previous morning. The huge crater had thrown mud and debris everywhere, damaging the electricity and water supply, smashing windows and putting the building where the hospital kitchen worked out of action. In the wards, beds had been hastily crowded into undamaged rooms, while some residents were forced to sleep in the corridors. Around nine hundred people had been in the hospital at the time, most of them alone, without any family members or anywhere else to go.

The director of the hospital department we were in, Olena, said that with basic safety to worry about, receiving the Food Train meals had been a godsend. 'At least we don't have to think about where to get a thousand portions of food.' She had overwhelmingly positive things to say about the experience. 'Most patients come from really low-income families, and the level and the quality of food they receive now from this train is so much better than they could have hoped for. It's maybe even the best we've seen for ten years.'

Back at the train, as the kitchen staff clambered on board after their break, I met Oleksii Shpionov, who had turned his Set Catering business over to World Central Kitchen at the start of the war and was still feeding more than a thousand people a day at his volunteer base in Irpin. They were then awarded the contract to carry out the food preparation on the Food Train. Despite an impossibly frenetic workload, he appeared to have enough energy to power an entire train by himself. 'Nobody ever thought what we were doing was possible, but already on the train we have cooked more than 400,000 meals, twice what was planned. The record for one day is 12,000,' he said proudly. The only thing currently stopping them from making twice as many portions was the packaging: if they had reusable containers, he said, they could easily increase their output to 20,000 meals a day. 'Even so, this train is so important, it is unique, for the budget we can cook and serve a huge amount of food per day.'

I asked about his experience working with World Central Kitchen, founded by the American chef José Andrés, which had become one of the most well respected overseas charities operating inside Ukraine. 'In most situations, they took their own staff who worked in the field as volunteers. But in Ukraine, they couldn't handle the sheer amount of help that was needed, so they decided to partner with local kitchens, including ourselves. They came to us and said we will take care of your budget, just do your thing, cook, we will cover everything.' At first, he said, he wanted to turn down the offer. 'Ukrainians are not used to someone offering to give you everything. We thought maybe they just wanted marketing to promote themselves. But then José said he didn't need any media, that they just wanted to help us do our work: "Please continue to cook," he said, "and we will support you." And that's how our story began.'

In the first year his volunteer kitchen in Irpin was feeding five or six thousand people a day. 'In a very gentle way, we are cutting out those people who now don't need our help: perhaps they found work, or they have some other support. We try to act efficiently and focus on the most vulnerable.' They hand out tickets to people for each week, which entitles them to meals at the kitchen, while they also try to encourage their guests not to depend entirely on humanitarian aid. 'We understood that if people just receive help all the time, they will become used to it, and that is not good for anyone. So once or twice a week we don't give out cooked meals, but packs of ingredients which they can prepare by themselves. So they will become more independent, without what we call this humanitarian addiction.'

After more than two years of war, when Ukrainians were exhausted and money was tight, raising funds remained a challenge. Shpionov and his team have sometimes organised events abroad, cooking Ukrainian food at big charity dinners in the West. He has been trying to rebuild his catering business too, to help cover the budget which he's been spending on all his volunteer projects. And family life is highly complicated: although his wife works as the kitchen team manager on board the Food Train, he can go months without seeing his sons. 'But for now we are here, in Kharkiv cooking for ten thousand people every day, and this is our important mission. The Buffett Foundation believed in us, and in Ukrainian Railways, and so we are leading this cool cooperation.' He reached over to the coffee machine to make another espresso. One of the chefs had prepared some staff food for the team, borsch and chicken Kyiv; I managed to snatch a few mouthfuls of it while we talked, but Shpionov had no time to eat. 'The head of Ukrainian Railways always looks out for us, if there is some bombing or explosions around this area, he always texts us to ask if we are OK. He is really invested in this whole project.' We talked about the previous railway boss Oleksandr Kamyshin again, the man who instilled the 'Keep Running' mentality into everything they did. 'He doesn't know the word no. It's always a yes for him, so I think that the Food Train project is really thanks to him, and his desire to create ambitious things like this. We always need to learn from such people, who believe in others and give them the opportunities they need.'

The train was about to get moving, there were supplies to pick up, orders to take and another menu to begin planning for the next day. 'When the war is over, this train could become an example for the whole world,' he said, and he had similar aspirations for the World Central Kitchen charity to which he had devoted so much of his life. 'We are not soldiers armed with weapons, but food is our weapon. We are food fighters, as José Andrés calls us. Chefs for Ukraine.'

Chapter Fourteen
EAT LOCAL

It's always been a relief to pull up at a Ukrainian petrol station. Not just to refuel the car, but to pick up a cup of strong filter coffee and a hot dog for the driver, the long sausages neatly poked into a specially hollowed-out bun, sometimes adorned with a smiley face drawn in mayonnaise. Ukraine is a vast country, and many of the ordinary citizens who turned into volunteers for the war effort have ended up driving thousands of miles to deliver supplies to the front lines. Volunteering has been a part of life for some Ukrainians since 2014 when Russian forces first invaded the eastern Donetsk and Luhansk regions and illegally annexed Crimea. People who had relatives in the armed forces began sending them medical supplies, thermal clothing, helmets and boots. But when the full-scale invasion happened, tens of thousands more people began doing what they could to help, collecting money for walkie-talkies and thermal vision scopes, body armour and tourniquets. On the long journeys east, in vans crammed to the roof with boxes, those petrol stations became a haven. Somehow, they remained supplied with an incredible variety of drinks and snacks, while the toilets were always pristine. The longer the war went on, and the further east you went, the more the other customers were almost exclusively military, snatching a last break on their way to the front.

One of the biggest petrol station chains, Okko, began giving soldiers free coffees and hot dogs, in dozens of branches across the front-line territories. They called it the 'Warm up Defenders' initiative and took donations for it online or at the till. Two years into the war, they estimated that they had given away 4.6 million coffees and 2.7 million hot dogs. Takeaway cups come decorated with a slogan – '*Oko na Oko*', or an eye for an eye, and a grinning mouth with teeth made from bullets. That initiative has raised millions of pounds for reconnaissance drones and air defence weapons. Petrol station staff are always ready to give soldiers a warm welcome, although they must have a stressful life themselves, working in such front-line locations. Once, while I was accompanying volunteers driving through the Donetsk region just before Christmas in 2022, the team had planned to make a stop at an Okko in Kostyantynivka on the way down towards Pokrovsk. As we drew up, we could see a large crater right near the forecourt where a missile had landed a few hours earlier. Fortunately no one had been injured, and construction workers were already on the scene, starting to clear up the damage. The petrol station opened up again within a couple of weeks. The free coffee scheme has been welcomed by soldiers, who have shown their appreciation, sometimes posting their thanks on social media. 'It's not about money, it's about respect,' wrote one man, 'and understanding that you are supported, that the war affects everyone.'

Helping the military has become part of doing business across the economy, and Ukraine's flair with technology has made it easy to deploy a simple process to support it. Ask for the bill at a cafe, and when you scan the QR code to pay, first there will be an option to give a tip, and then with another click you can donate to a fund helping the military.

When you buy a train ticket, you can not only order your morning cup of tea in advance, but you can also pay for one for a Ukrainian defender. Long queues quickly formed when McDonald's Ukraine reopened their doors in a few cities, eight months after the invasion. But with less fanfare, the firm's charity arm has donated hundreds of thousands of meal kits to families in liberated or front-line territories, and donated money from cheeseburger sales to the bombed Okhmatdyt children's hospital in Kyiv.

Big businesses have been forced to adapt incredibly rapidly to the challenges of wartime conditions, in the effort to keep critical services functioning. Supermarkets have had to be especially resilient, as they worked out how to keep their shelves stocked with produce when all the usual supply routes suddenly ground to a halt. Since February 2022, they've lost stores and warehouses to shelling or occupation and faced catastrophic energy cuts. Silpo, which is part of the giant Fozzy group, lost millions of pounds as soon as the full-scale war broke out, after dozens of stores ended up in occupied areas, or were situated in places where it was too dangerous to remain open. According to Ukrainian government site DIA, stores and distribution warehouses came under shelling, or were looted by Russian occupiers. Immediately after the invasion, the company went into a state of crisis management, planning for a few days ahead at a time, and finding new ways to transport goods around the country. Importing products from abroad was even more of a challenge, with no airports, and Black Sea ports out of action. By turning to their network of local suppliers, all the supermarket groups managed to keep an impressive array of produce available, although the more expensive ranges have been priced out of many people's reach. While it's been a challenge for industry giants like the Fozzy group, it's left small businesses with less of a financial safety net struggling to survive one crisis after another.

Hundreds of thousands of men volunteered for the armed forces or were mobilised, while millions of women and children who left the country have yet to return. Two years into the war, businesses have often struggled to fill jobs. One cafe owner I met voiced her frustration in an Instagram post which went viral: we have no people at all, she wrote. 'Soon we will end up with just ten items on the menu, with just two waiters at a time in place of ten... badly made cappuccino and under-seasoned omelette. Our business will stop.' By the spring of 2024, another regime of energy blackouts brought yet more worries for small producers. On top of everything else, they were forced to use generators powered by expensive diesel fuel, with no way to maintain a consistent power supply.

But the Silpo supermarket chain has motored on, keeping schemes going like the Lavka Traditsiia, or Shop of Traditions. The initiative was designed to seek out quality products from small producers and farmers in different parts of the country, and help them to get into selected stores. Marina Bulatska, who's in charge of the scheme, told me how it started – and how it has adapted to war. 'Twenty years ago, we understood that somewhere within Ukrainian customers, part of our cultural DNA, is to buy basic fresh products like cottage cheese or cured meat at the market,' she said. 'You want something fresh from the village, so that's where you should go, to see your favourite lady at the market and chat to her. But you don't know anything about the logistics, where she makes it and how. So we decided to add the element of quality control, all the certificates to underscore food security – and to create this feeling of going to market, inside our stores.'

The retail chain decided to focus on five of the country's major cities and began with a section showcasing a dozen or so producers inside one of their most upmarket Le Silpo stores – which carry a more specialist range of goods than the standard Silpo branches. 'We had some basic products: cottage cheese, milk, local cheesecake called *zapekanka*, and some cured meat. Then honey, jam and herbal tea. Then year after year, we began to expand the range.' They had to overcome what she calls a widespread stereotype, that supermarkets were all about marketing and profits: 'They are just evil, there's nothing good.' Instead, she insists, they wanted to foster a culture of local consumption, as well as supporting small Ukrainian producers. 'Let's take one case. We found a small, full-circle farm, and a farmer who makes three- and six-month-old cheese. We didn't have a producer in this category, so we invited him to help build it with us. For him, it helped to develop his business because we committed to certain volumes, and for us, we had found a good partner, and we knew the quality was high. We have our own cheese technology expert, and so he went there to work on it, to make sure all the processes were good.' She says the scheme helps small producers with the things they can't manage by themselves. 'We understand that not all farmers have their own logistics. But we have a huge network, four storage warehouses around the country, transport, the whole chain.' Partners in the scheme sign an exclusive relationship with the company for that product, with its own branding and packaging. 'Maybe it is a bit risky to work with one retailer, but we try to build a transparent relationship and they know that tomorrow – I hope – we won't close our doors. It offers them some stability.'

The most common worry was volume and scale. 'They tell us – I am scared, I can't produce enough, you are a big chain. But we reassure them that it's OK. You can start in just one store, three, five, whatever. I'm a big fan of local heroes. We can have one range in Lviv, and it will be totally different from one in central Ukraine.'

When the full-scale war began, having a ready network of local suppliers was suddenly an unexpected bonus, and customers who tried their produce found they enjoyed it more than they anticipated. While imported goods became much more expensive after, local goods are now often discounted to boost demand. 'We have different price tags: the regular one is white and special offers are yellow, and this yellow tag is like magic for increasing sales.' For years, Silpo had tried to attract more customers by holding weekly 'market days', inviting farmers and producers into bigger stores. 'We had tastings and gave people an opportunity to meet the producer, to ask questions and have a special offer as well.' All that was suspended when the war broke out, but by the summer of 2024 they had resumed again, with a series of two-day food festivals around the country called True and Local. One initiative included a trip to a goat farm near Kyiv so that customers could really see behind the scenes. 'People were saying they'd never seen cheese being made before, the whole day was full of emotions. We decided to let them try making mozzarella themselves; we all did it together – it was crazy. After this one day, all of them turned into real advocates for our brands. It is really powerful, on a different level to advertising with videos.'

With no cheap small business loans from banks or the government, giving their partners some help with marketing and development has proved even more crucial. 'There are two types of farmers and producers here. Some still have a lot of money from previous businesses, to invest in equipment and new technology. And the second used to work in other industries, but they quit to start something new and small.

They created their own paths, from their home kitchens; their businesses are about herbal teas or candies or jams. For them it is much harder to grow, because you need to constantly generate demand.'

She says it can be hard to build awareness about the importance of marketing, 'because when they are in their kitchens, they think only "we made this with our own hands!" Inside the stores, unfortunately, customers don't really think about how much hard work was involved in the process, they just want to buy some chocolate. If you can't tell the story about your chocolate, I'm sorry, it's hard.'

As part of Lavka Traditsiia, the company set up a school for food entrepreneurs, covering everything from quality control to marketing. They took the classes online during the pandemic, and then when the war broke out, the format went hybrid, with some lectures in person and others staying online. They got funding to provide ten producers with free places. 'I knew that not every student would end up on our shelves. So, we need to think about different ways of distribution: you can work with a small cafe, you can develop e-commerce, you can do projects like a special delivery box, or sell to other businesses. This really opened people's eyes, and the marketing module became the most popular one we ran.' The course on sustainability has turned into one about survival during war. 'People are exhausted, they need to hear about inspiring things.'

I took the long drive south from Kharkiv to Kremenchuk in central Ukraine, to a workshop run by two brothers who have been making hand-crafted organic chocolate for more than a decade.

In a concrete outbuilding between a main road and a block of flats, they do everything themselves. From roasting the cocoa beans and extracting the nibs, to conching it into smooth, luxurious chocolate and tempering it into bars. They have come up with a wild array of flavours, including one with parmesan cheese, an experimental one with donkey milk, and some low-sugar bars sweetened with spices and freeze-dried berries. Their labels are decorated with beautiful designs by a local artist, based on traditional Ukrainian symbols.

When Oleksii and Dima started Meetty with a tiny roasting oven which they had bought online from India, there was hardly anyone in Ukraine making bean-to-bar chocolate from scratch. Dima, who had previously worked as an economist, taught himself all the techniques by watching videos on YouTube. They set out to use as many local products as possible, along with cocoa beans which are mostly sourced from the Caribbean, and have managed to keep their organic certification intact. Oleksii said the Good Wine Company in Kyiv had given them a lot of business support when they first started out. 'They gave us a lot of suggestions about what to do in terms of our new production, because they had many years of experience. So we learned a lot from them.' From selling bars in Good Wine, Meetty formed partnerships with other small brands, and then a large organic milk company which wanted to use their chocolate to cover their curd cheese bars, a popular snack for children.

Dressed in an overall and protective shoes, Oleksii began showing my friend Masha and me around the small production unit where three conching machines were whirring away, filling the air with the irresistible aroma of melting chocolate. Suddenly the entire room was plunged into darkness and everything stopped: the city's rolling blackout had kicked in. Dima rushed outside to fetch some diesel and get the generator started, while we continued our mini tour with the light from Oleksii's phone torch. The conching machines, which grind the cocoa nibs into smooth chocolate paste, need to be kept on all the time, and at a constant temperature, otherwise the entire process will be spoiled. 'We can't afford to have everything running on this generator. So, we have to choose,' Oleksii said. 'And if the power shuts down at night, during the curfew, we can't come out here to turn the generator on.' To get around it, the ever-ingenious Dima had managed to rig up a system which would allow him to start it up from home. 'It's still very expensive to have all these accumulators and inverters. We bought a big generator which we can switch on automatically. Dima made a special gadget to switch it on from a distance, because we just have to manage in this new environment. We have some very demanding clients.'

In the chaotic weeks after the full-scale invasion, it had become impossible to get the labels printed for their chocolate bars. 'The printers told us – guys, you're mad. We can't make anything without electricity. The only printing we could get was really bad quality. And one of our clients just insisted that they needed their product on time. OK, it's war, they said to us – but come on, we still have to do our jobs.' Once things were a bit more stable they contacted a well-known artist, Sergiy Maidukov, who agreed to design a special range of labels for them with splashes of bold primary colours in his trademark modernist style. Another illustrator helped with their range of low-sugar chocolate for children, with designs based on Ukrainian fairy tales – which Oleksii thought had a very contemporary message for families who had been traumatised by everything they had been through. 'There is a story behind this; it is about trust, about a feeling of safety, about justice.'

Dima tipped a large bowl of melted chocolate onto a marble worktop and began tempering it, rhythmically pushing the chocolate around with a scraper, so that it made undulating waves. Every few seconds he would check the temperature with a digital thermometer and as soon as it had cooled down to the exact point he wanted, he deftly scraped it all back into the bowl, then weighed it into the moulds they use for their bars, exactly 80 grams for each one. It was hot weather and I wondered aloud how they managed to store the bars without a working fridge. 'We just send them off to customers as soon as we've made them – then trying to keep them without melting isn't our problem,' Oleksii said.

He unwrapped a selection of chocolates so that we could try them, fanning them out on a table under the dim glow of the phone torch. He began talking about his recent trip to the front lines with volunteers taking food and supplies to injured soldiers in hospitals. They had brought a dentist with them, he said, who had offered his services to the soldiers for free. Most of his volunteering work had been with a charity fund which builds temporary new homes for people who have been displaced from their homes in Chernihiv region, along with bomb shelters for people living near the Russian border. 'In one village we put up ten homes and two shelters – it isn't a lot but it is very effective. So this is how I spend the main part of my working hours.' Such is the life of a Ukrainian entrepreneur during war.

We managed to eat our way through a surprising number of chocolate bars – the one with parmesan was unexpectedly my favourite – and then ventured out into the city centre, where generators were keeping the power going in a row of restaurants. We shared some plates of salad and a cube-shaped mousse dessert with pear jam and chocolate inside, which was called *Slava Ukraini*, sprayed in a vivid blue and yellow glaze. Oleksii led us on a walk down to the banks of the wide Dnipro river, and although it was far too dark to see very much, there were little patches of light where men were fishing down on the shore. I left, loaded up with boxes of chocolate bars on the night train back to Kyiv, hoping it wouldn't melt in the fierce heat of the sleeper compartment top bunk.

Back in the capital, I went to visit a young confectioner called Maria Timoshenko, who switched to using Meetty chocolate to make her range of filled chocolate bars and fudge, after discovering that the Belgian brand she had been using still operated in Russia. Maria had chosen the confectionary life after leaving her old career in marketing behind. 'I had a kind of emotional crisis and left my job and went to work in a coffee shop. I became a barista and thought that I might create a place where you could try all sorts of different coffees and match them with cheese. I thought it was a really cool idea, but I couldn't make it work because I didn't have any contacts or cooking experience.' So she took courses in food technology and started making fudge at home, creating flavours which she would enjoy herself.

At first she sold her sweets to friends, then through social media and word of mouth – and then someone from Kyiv's Good Wine shop tried it, and approved. They got in touch to say they wanted to sell it in their city-centre delicatessen, which turned out to be the lucky career break she needed. For seven years she grew her business, boosting sales with her spiky personality on her social media accounts, which won her a growing audience of loyal fans.

The challenges of operating in wartime brought another level of stress as the cost of ingredients soared, along with fuel, but there was a limit to how far she could raise the price of her confectionary. 'We understand that for every

Ukrainian their first priority if they have money to spare is to donate to the army, not for non-essential goods like chocolate. But we are still very glad that there are people who manage to do both.' She created an online option on her own website where customers could buy a bar of chocolate for a Ukrainian soldier, which was sent out by postal delivery. One of her own staff members, a girl who had been her first chocolatier, had decided to join the armed forces. 'A year ago, she volunteered to go to the Azov Brigade as a combat medic. We still make a special chutney using her recipe.' Maria developed a special bar in a collaboration with the military charity Come Back Alive, filled with apple jam, caramel and cinnamon, which echoed the comforting flavours of apple pie, and pledged to hand over 100 per cent of the profits to one of the charity's initiatives.

She had to learn how to manage with the relentless blackouts which made running her specialist equipment almost impossible. 'When there is no power, the machines which are tempering the chocolate shut down, but they need to keep going constantly for two or three days because if the chocolate gets too cold and hard it won't melt like it should.' On her birthday, she says, her friends clubbed together and raised enough money for her to buy a generator. 'It means we can keep the lights on, the fridge, the induction hob, although there isn't enough power to work the boiler for the jam.' It has become a case of constantly juggling her priorities within the limits of what is physically possible.

Since the power was still working on the afternoon when I visited with Edward, a photographer friend, Maria was busy making a batch of raspberry and lime jam with crates of fruit from the market. On some shelves at the back of the room there were trays of fudge ready to be cut up and packaged. She urged me to try some, and with slightly indecent haste we sliced into a batch of chocolate fudge, rich and velvety, then some with cubes of Dutch cheese inside, and another flecked with lemon and poppy seed. Maria brought out some bars of chocolate, filled with hazelnut praline and gingerbread with orange, breaking them open on a small round table which had a message almost hidden in the mosaic 'F— off Russia'. 'It's hard for me,' she said, 'but I love this job, even the monotony of it, and it has really helped me to fight my depression.'

A recent small business award from the Kyiv School of Economics came just when she needed it. 'It became three times more expensive to do everything because of the cost of fuel,' she said, 'and if you apply for any government help it will take two or three months for them to reply.' The KSE grant, she said, had gone towards some new equipment she had needed. With her father and her brother both in the Ukrainian armed forces, she made her military fundraisers a priority, all the while dreaming up new chocolate recipes, keeping up a constant presence on social media and managing her kitchen operation day by day. 'So many husbands, brothers, fathers went to war, that women are now the ones running businesses,' she said. And more than rising to the challenge.

On a blazing hot day at the beginning of September 2024, I met up with Silpo's Marina Bulatska again, at the company's first True and Local festival since the full-scale invasion. It had been set up in a large courtyard behind a cafe and exhibition space in Kyiv's Podil district, and despite the heatwave, there were plenty of hot-food vendors, jostling for space with coffee and juice stands. Around the edge there were stalls showcasing a large range of Lavka Traditsiia products, from local cheeses and smoked meats to jams and candied fruit. The focus of the festival, however, was bread, with a huge display in the middle of the courtyard featuring dozens of traditional Ukrainian loaves with labels explaining the history behind each one. Some of the city's best sourdough bakeries had been given stalls, and were handing out samples of *palyanytsya* bread, dark rye and sweet pastries for people to try. There were young couples with children, a DJ was playing music, and some chefs were roasting plums on the edge of a fire pit for a special dinner, with flames curling around the charcoal, the heady smell of charring, caramelised sugar and fruit.

It was a small miracle that such events could still happen at such a difficult time for the city, with frequent blackouts and nightly attacks. In the early hours of that morning, twenty Russian missiles targeted Kyiv, the sound of explosions sending people scrambling into corridors or bathrooms, emergency shelter in the darkness before dawn. It seemed unbelievable that amid such challenges, anyone was managing to make a small business work at all, but here were people trying to do it both sustainably and right. I remembered what Marina had told me as we walked between the stalls, talking to the producers about their work. 'Sustainability is not just about the future, but part of our cultural code,' she said. 'It is about working like this day by day – for life.'

Part Four

HOPE

FOOD CULTURE & HERITAGE

Chapter Fifteen

FROM FOREST DINNERS TO KYIV COOL

In a forest, two hours outside Kyiv, a group of chefs were basting cherries with slabs of butter and smashing aubergines into a flat circular hotplate which surrounded a blazing fire. The air smelled of damp pine trees and wood smoke and the musky aftermath of rain. It was the summer of 2023, when Kyiv had become better protected by air defence, but it was always impossible to escape the sounds of war. You could make out the odd muffled explosion in the background, and it was hard to tell whether this was from demining teams or training exercises. 'Don't worry about those, it's our boys.'

This clearing, with its fire pit, its outdoor prep kitchen and long dining table carefully laid for dinner under the canopy of trees, was the setting for one of chef Igor Mezencev's monthly events which he had created to keep connected with the bounty of Ukrainian land. He had a regular group of friends who were part of these Forest Dinners: his food photographer Dima, a young man called Konstantin who was a foraging expert, and for this dinner he had invited a fermentation specialist called Dasha who knew all about pickling and preserving. When we arrived, Igor was sitting on some upturned boxes, steadily preparing cherries and threading them onto long skewers, ready to be roasted in their bath of butter. Another young chef was busy wrapping beef fillet in dough, like a kind of Wellington, and then covering the whole thing in a tight parcel of foil, so that it could be cooked directly on the embers. There were balls of cooked cornmeal, stuffed with pork and fried in oil like croquettes, sizzling away in their copper saucepans on the edge of the fire. There was a huge flat pan balanced on an iron tripod over the flames, full of onions and tomatoes cooking down into a rich sauce. Plums and peaches were being roasted around the edge for dessert. While Dima handed out small cups of buckwheat tea, Konstantin led us down into the woods and along the banks of a small river to find herbs and flowers which could be used in the meal. He had an encyclopaedic knowledge of native plants, most of which I had never come across before, and kept darting off into the undergrowth and emerging again with bundles of leaves. We scrambled back through the remnants of an unseasonal summer rainstorm, arms full of edible herbs, the finishing touches for the dinner.

Sitting around the table with the other guests, under slightly dripping trees, we watched Dasha give a demonstration on how to prepare a sunflower as if it were artichoke, trimming off the tough leaves and stem until a small disc of the edible part was left. A pickled version turned up on the starter, scattered with some of Konstantin's herbs. The smashed aubergines were served over the gently cooked stew of onion and tomato, with the odd burst of smoky, roasted plum. The cornmeal fritters were crunchy but soft and savoury inside, and the roasted peaches, almost collapsing into their own juice, were the perfect dessert with some cream sweetened with foraged herbs which had an echo of tonka, or vanilla.

Igor Mezencev, a towering presence of a man with a decidedly impish smile, had begun his drive to get Ukrainian chefs reconnected to the land years before the full-scale invasion. He set up a project called Topot, taking young chefs out into the Carpathian mountains and challenging them to cook using only the ingredients they could find. 'For maybe a year, I was learning about mushrooms and plants. I was scared to go on my own to the forest and try to survive there for five or six days,' he remembers. At first no one wanted to join his trips to live off foraged food. 'Nobody said it was a good idea, they all said they had no time. So, we started looking for people who were not famous restaurant chefs, but who had some experience or knowledge about wild plants. And so we collected a team for the first Topot, and when we were all together as a team, all my fears about the forest left me. There was only one way to go.' He had been trying to dream up the food of the future, but realised he needed to go back to where it all began. 'I think if you really go back to the roots, how people first cooked meat or vegetables in the fire, surviving in the forest, your brain will start working in a new way.'

In February 2022, he was living in Kharkiv, working on his Topot plans and cooking at a restaurant in the city. He lived in a flat in Saltivka, an area which immediately came under relentless bombardment as Russian forces advanced towards the city. On the day of the invasion, he posted an urgent message on his Instagram: 'Russia attacked us early this morning. I want chefs around the world to know this! I am writing this text lying on the cold floor, and the electricity and water have already been turned off... I can hear only explosions around.' It became impossible to get out to buy food, and there were constant blackouts. Igor began cooking as best he could, with the contents of his rapidly defrosting freezer. After living like this for a hundred days under shelling, he started posting a kind of culinary diary on social media. 'They say that everyone has aged about fifteen or twenty years. I think we lost fear here, not our youth. And for me, it is even worse, you just stop thinking about your life, or rather, you only think about the day you woke up.' He resolved to post a series of twenty photos of his old family recipes, written in the Ukrainian language and reimagined in restaurant style. He devised a spreadsheet called the Victory Menu and tried to get friends in the industry involved. He thought it might become a resource for chefs around the world to start celebrating Ukrainian cooking. There was borsch made with smoked pear, and roasted cabbage which had first been left outside overnight in the frost, so that the ice would break it down, then baked in the oven until it was almost melting, with butter and spices. There were corn cobs first baked, then fried on the fire, decorated with fried scraps of *salo* and pickled rose petals. And a childhood dessert: puff pastry cornets filled with whipped cream and caramelised condensed milk, scattered with toasted nuts.

Eventually he decided that trying endlessly to perfect well-known dishes like borsch and *varenyky* would lead him down a dead end. He moved from Kharkiv to Kyiv and ended up taking charge of the kitchen at a five-star hotel, the Fairmont. 'I found myself looking for some kind of switch, to restart my outlook on Ukrainian cuisine, because I wanted to show that it doesn't just exist in our imagination.' He decided that although he could play around with the basics, he would turn his focus to the land. 'In my opinion, this whole process goes through three generations. First, we try to remake our old recipes. Second, we make a twist on these old classics. Take *shuba*, which is a layered dish of beetroot, potato and herring – we could make it lighter and use salmon instead. Or we could make Olivier potato salad with fresh crab. And thirdly, the new way, is to work with produce direct from the farm, or from the forest.'

At the hotel he was given the opportunity to try out some of his new ideas. 'Hotels are the first places which people see when they arrive in Ukraine. So it should be a place where we can really showcase the coolest and the best Ukrainian cuisine. We should create perfect dishes in the old style, but we can add some more modern ideas to the menu too, all using Ukrainian produce.' It was early spring, and his hotel kitchen had plenty of vegetables on order: young cabbages, tomatoes, asparagus and wild garlic. 'We have some rules here, that we can only work with Ukrainian farmers. If I want *burrata* on the menu, I have to find a Ukrainian version, not just buy Italian cheese. I want to show what we can do with all this seasonal produce which our farmers grow.' He also wanted to champion the creativity of young chefs who had trained in places like Denmark and Japan, and were now using the techniques they learned there with the home-grown ingredients they could find in Ukraine. He offered to arrange a special 'gastronomic tour' for me, around Kyiv, a project which he had been working on since before the war, focusing on showing people the best and most modern examples of traditional Ukrainian food. This time, he rightly assumed that with my incorrigible sweet tooth, I would want to concentrate on pastries and desserts. 'Just me and you, we will go to see all the cool bakeries, you will find out what people here can do.' He sent over a schedule; I had imagined a single day, perhaps just a morning, but he had planned an entire week of visits. There was going to be a lot of pastry.

We began at a small coffee shop on a side street off another side street, 16 Coffee. They took their pastries from a small wholesale bakery called Pate Kyiv, and as we arrived a young woman was unpacking that day's delivery into the display case. There were croissants, baked into golden swirls with raisins or pistachio paste, and custard tarts in crisp, laminated pastry crusts, cinnamon buns and *pain suisse*, and *canelé* burnished to a deep bronze. We tried a selection: a slab of carrot cake with cream cheese icing, and most excitingly, a large wedge of panettone soaked in a citrus syrup and baked again with almond frangipane. From there we walked to the Podil district and Spelta, run by Iliya Syomin and Olga Hrynchuk, with its ultra-modern, Scandinavian vibe. Iliya had spent time working in Copenhagen with Richard Hart, a British baker who had gone from working at the three-Michelin-star NOMA to opening his own bakery in the city and became one of the most influential people in the modern sourdough world. The pastries at Spelta were excellent: light and crisp, shattering into flaky shards as Igor cut them into halves. Iliya showed us around the narrow open kitchen and sent us on our way with a star-shaped loaf of buckwheat sourdough and some jars of his home-made 'Kyiv Kraut'.

Not far from Spelta was Zavertailo, another destination cafe, run by one of the city's culinary power couples, Stanislav and Anna Zavertailo. At a cosy table inside, they promptly ordered a large selection of twice-baked croissants and a strawberry Kyiv cake. There was a special 'Boris Johnson' pastry, filled with apple and custard and topped with a rakish quiff of meringue, in the style of the former prime minister's unkempt hair. Zavertailo – and their other site, the Honey Cafe – had become well known for creating highly sought after desserts, while raising hundreds of thousands of pounds to help the Ukrainian armed forces in the process. He swept us into a taxi across town to his production unit, a hive of workshops each dedicated to a single product. We peered into the first room, where staff were making filled chocolates shaped like the famous rooster jug which survived a missile strike in Borodyanka. In another space, bakers were making perfect-looking choux buns and eclairs. Across the corridor in the bread bakery, there were bagels and panettone on the go; Stanislav selected one from a cooling shelf, studded with dried fruit and candied peel, and sliced it in half to check the crumb, passing us pieces to try. He was working on a new dessert, based around sea buckthorn, a berry which is said to have healing powers. It looked like a sprig of wild berries, but inside were intricate layers of vanilla mousse, pecan praline and sea buckthorn jam with ginger and lime. It was all a hugely impressive sight.

The next morning Igor met me bright and early again as I scurried to keep up with his stride through yet another part of the Podil district. We hurried past the bright pink Namelaka cafe, bedecked in flowers, with its cabinets full of intricate layered cakes and choux buns, to a small industrial unit where Vlad Marchuk and his wife Yuliia had their production bakery. 'We started work on this space more than a year ago,' Yuliia said, as we walked inside. 'It was a time when there were the most intense rocket attacks. So, we had to do most of the work by ourselves. I was painting here, Vlad was building walls.'

Vlad had been one of the original members of Mezencev's Topot team back in 2019, trekking into the depths of the forest and building an oven from scratch to bake bread. He had lugged thirty kilograms of flour in his backpack up the mountains, getting up before dawn each day to get the dough ready. 'I was so proud of Vlad,' Yuliia says. 'It is unreal to make an oven and bake bread, right in the middle of the woods.' Before the big war, he had helped to start a bakery group called Khlebnyi. It had grown rapidly from a single small site to more than twenty cafes, and Vlad was nicknamed 'Professor', with a reputation for constantly dreaming up something new. 'But we were always hoping to find a place where we could have our own dream, our small factory. We finally found this place, and wanted the project to be something really special, so we decided to use only local Ukrainian products.' While they were walking their dog around the area, they noticed wild hops were growing. 'A hundred years ago here, it was common for people to use hop shoots in their sourdough starter. So, we decided to bring back that old tradition.' They had been baking their bread with a starter which they'd kept going for seven years. But while Kyiv was coming under such frequent attack, no one had time to look after it, and they had to begin again. 'We mixed these wild hops and water with our flour, and put lots of love into it, and created our new Podil starter. Soon it will be two years old, and it is like a piece of history. It is so important to bring back our traditions.'

Vlad had laid a table with some of his latest croissants for us to try, which he had been developing for the Idealist coffee shop chain. There was one filled with poppy seed paste and cherries, and another made from dough that had been laminated with herb butter, green swirls around salty *brinza* cheese. There was a sturdy fruit loaf, reimagined from a childhood recipe. We left loaded down with brioche buns and slices of leftover cake. Everything flavoured with that special Podil starter, a piece of local history in every slice.

We took the ever-reliable metro, which has remarkably kept running more or less as normal, the stations so deep underground they serve as bomb shelters during missile alarms. We got out at Arsenalna, near the government headquarters, and just beyond the bustling Kyiv Food Market building was a small restaurant called Bavovna. The name – Ukrainian for cotton, as well as 'bang' in Russian – was a reference to a popular wartime joke, and the young chef in charge, Dmitry Kryvoshap, had worked at a couple of two-Michelin-star restaurants, Inua in Tokyo and Alchemist in Copenhagen. The space was tiny, spread over two floors, with an open-fire kitchen on the ground floor. Dmitry bounded upstairs to our table bearing a loaf of their crusty sourdough bread, served with three kinds of butter. His food was intricate and beautifully composed: my favourite dish was a wedge of roasted pumpkin over fermented plums, with crunchy shards of Ukrainian hazelnuts and roasted seaweed chips, and a sauce made from smoked courgettes. For dessert, Igor asked him to bring over a plate of his crispy waffles with home-made cherry jam and ice cream, as well as the signature Bavovna dessert: biscuits made to a recipe by Dmitry's grandmother, cooked on the open flame, sandwiched with toasted marshmallow and the instruction, 'Eat it with your hands.'

We spent the last morning back in Igor's kitchen in the Fairmont hotel, where his pastry chef Eduard was busy rolling out sheets of laminated dough and pulling sourdough loaves out of the oven. We tried some dark rye bread, croissants filled with chocolate, and pastry swirls filled with raisins and poppy seed, while Igor talked about his next Forest Dinner plans and a book about Topot which was soon to be published, in collaboration with his photographer, Dima. 'It will be in Ukrainian and English, so I will send you one!' He dashed off again and emerged with an intricate loaf made of individual spirals of root vegetables, placed perfectly in waves, all the colours of the rainbow. 'I don't want to just make old European recipes, even if they are very popular with people, because there is nowhere for a chef to grow. I want to show that modern Ukrainian cuisine doesn't just exist in our imagination. That's why I have taken you to see what we really have, all this amazing bread and these beautiful croissants – this is a new way to really show the world what we can do.'

Chapter Sixteen
WELCOME TO BESSARABIA

At the military checkpoint, around half an hour outside Odesa, every non-commercial vehicle is waved to a stop by the side of the road. There are minibuses, private cars and vans, all pulled up on the hard shoulder in a queue stretching back for a couple of hundred yards. Soldiers walk up and down, asking for documents which they take away to make their many checks and double checks. Up on the main road, hundreds of lorries are busy rumbling past, because what looks like a nondescript highway is in fact the only remaining road from southern Ukraine into the European Union, a vital supply route for export goods like food and grain. The only other road was blocked off in the early months of the war when Russian forces bombed a key road and rail bridge along the coast at Zatoka, and since then the newly strategic Danube ports of Izmail and Reni have been under relentless Russian drone attack, night after night for more than two years. Despite Russia's decision to abandon the agreement to honour a safe grain corridor in the Black Sea, as well as blockades by farmers across the Polish border, Ukrainian food and grain exports managed to bounce back by the end of 2023, although they were still below pre-war levels. Agri-food exports on their own were worth just under twelve and a half billion dollars in the first half of 2024, a 5 per cent increase on the same period the year before.

To reach southern Bessarabia, traffic must take the remaining road which technically transits through foreign territory, across the border in neighbouring Moldova. The frontier post at Palanca lies on the right of the highway, barricaded off behind a high metal fence, with the lights inside its solitary duty-free shop appealing to passing drivers to buy Moldovan products. Once all the various documents and permissions have been approved at the military checkpoint, you are allowed onwards, to join the stream of lorries on the main road which snakes around the Black Sea coast, towards this south-eastern enclave which has become home to a myriad of nationalities and cultures, and a heritage which is fiercely treasured and celebrated at every opportunity. You can tell what nationality a Bessarabian village is from the very shape of its architecture; the Gagauz homes look different from the Bulgarian or Romanian ones. The food and the customs are all different too – although nowadays there are Ukrainian flags everywhere, flashes of blue and yellow fluttering between the fence posts and the rooftops, above the Soviet-era monuments and along the walkways beside the coast. For all the multi-ethnic identities, the different languages and traditions in a place which has been variously controlled over the past two hundred years by the Ottoman and Russian empires, by the Moldovans, by Romania and the USSR, there is no mistaking where loyalty now lies, and Bessarabia is proudly Ukraine.

This is agricultural land, much of it still farmed by smallholders who typically own a few fields around their homes, where they can grow fruit and vegetables, raise goats and sheep and poultry. The rolling steppe with its rich soil, together with the humid summer climate, has created the ideal terroir for vines, with a flourishing wine-making industry – and a high quality which has helped wineries like Shabo and Kolonist to win awards and sell Ukrainian wines around the world. But the best-kept secret of Bessarabia is its legendary hospitality: to enter any of these villages is to be instantly welcomed into local homes.

It isn't the easiest place to get to: as well as the blockposts, away from the main highway the roads are a virtual assault course of potholes which have grown so large they merge into huge gashes across the surface, forcing cars into a kind of zigzag action, sometimes making them veer off course altogether onto an 'alternative road' dirt track through a nearby field. My first trip there was with my friend Maria, who had a huge passion for Bessarabian food and culture. She had just started organising gastronomic tours to the area when the full-scale invasion closed tourism down, and she was keen for me to meet some of the families who had hosted her guests. We drove into the small village of Plakhtiivka, and drew up at a small home, where a lady rushed out to greet us like old friends. She invited us in 'just for a cup of tea', which involved being ushered into a summer kitchen in the backyard. A table was hastily laid with plates of cucumber and tomato from the garden, carrots and spring onions pulled from the ground, cleaned of soil, huge bunches of fresh parsley and dill, bowls of dried fish and sausage, and salty local cheese. There was wine, and home-made spirits decanted into old fizzy pop bottles, for there should always be something to make a toast. And fragrant, sticky rose petal jam to eat with biscuits, which the family also made themselves.

It was a pretty substantial meal, but less than an hour later we were in the beautiful village of Krynychne to visit another local couple, Kirill and Tatyana, who were known for their wicked sense of humour and excellent home-baking skills. While Kirill told naughty jokes, Tatyana piled her kitchen table with many kinds of bread: brioche-style enriched loaves swirled with quince jam or poppy seed, a darker rye and a large white loaf made to share, a round pan of leftover sourdough filled with salty *brinza* cheese and served with honey and herbs. She constantly worried aloud that we would have nothing to eat. We went back for another visit, when she had baked a huge array of special *paska* bread using her sourdough starter – slicing into the biggest one to reveal the soft, buttery crumb inside. Tatyana's baking was something you would want to return for again and again.

A year later I was back in Bessarabia, to see how people had managed to keep their farms and businesses going. We called in at the home of Paskovia Trandahilova, who insisted we call her Pasha as she threw open the large gate into her yard. Built in the Bulgarian style, it formed an elongated single-storey L shape with outbuildings along the far side and a metal fence for vines. In a small brick building at the back of the yard, she was making paprika, drying out home-grown red peppers and pounding them into a fine, scarlet powder. But it was in the loft above the house where the real work was happening: up there, stored under the rafters, are tonnes of the tiny local onions called *arpazhik*. Growing them is incredibly hard work: the crops get planted in the plot behind the house during spring, and then whole families turn out in late August to harvest them by hand. Then they get cleaned and dried and carried up a steep staircase on the side of the house into the loft, ready to be sorted by size and then carefully stored.

Inside, there was a single light bulb and a fan to keep the air dry, while Pasha emptied a bucket of onions onto a large wire tray, scooping through it with her hands to get rid of any debris and make sure everything was clean. Her family has been growing these for longer than she can remember, she said – for more than seventy years. It has provided a decent source of income, although the price has plummeted since the full-scale war began; but like everything here, they continue working because this is their life, and there is no other option.

The light bulb threw strange shadows through the loft; in the semi-darkness, the long trays of onions gave off a soft, golden glow. Pasha filled a couple of plastic bags as a gift, for you can leave no home here empty handed, and turned back to her mounds of tiny *arpazhik*, tipping out yet another pail to be meticulously checked and sorted through by size again. Beneath the roofs of Krynychne, there are hidden treasure troves of gold.

We moved on to the home of Maria Nikolaevna and Fyodor Konstantin, where although it was not yet noon, things were already getting lively. They were all wearing traditional Bulgarian dress, ready to celebrate an annual wine makers' holiday known as Tryphon Zarezan or St Tryphon's Day, and Fyodor and his neighbour were eagerly beckoning us through the kitchen and into the small cellar. The walls were lined with rows of pickles and preserves: jars filled with cherry plums and watermelon, with quince and apricot and strawberries. Fyodor leapt into action with a length of plastic pipe, plunging it into a barrel and expertly syphoning off exactly the right amount of wine to fill a glass jug. Back outside in the yard, they had set up a small table underneath the vines coiled along the side of the house; there was a round flatbread, baked simply with flour and water, a tray of wine glasses and some secateurs. There was a centuries-old ritual to follow: the men ceremonially pruned the vine, while

Maria, in her maroon and plaid dress and sleeveless sheepskin jacket, carefully rolled the circular flatbread along the vines like a wheel, as if she wanted every piece of it to touch the living branch, then broke off pieces of the bread for everyone to taste. After that she poured wine over the vine and handed the rest of that around too while she dedicated a blessing. A cat ran about, dodging the drips of wine, while behind the house, they kept goats, a few pigs and sheep; at the back of one pen a fluffy black kid, born earlier that day, staggered to its feet, shuddering slightly at the shock of it all.

This day is set aside to mark the start of the agricultural season, and these carefully preserved traditions are supposed to ensure a great harvest later in the year. Before the war, it was an excuse for a giant street party: the whole village would turn out with music and dancing, everyone dressed in embroidered shirts and headscarves or black felt hats, crowning a king with a wicker wreath to celebrate the holiday of wine. In 2024, things were necessarily far more muted, but these villages were still determined to show that life and wine making could still go on.

One of the most energetic local businesses was Balkansyi Yastiia, a family-run enterprise in the village of Bolhrad which makes cured meat, pickles and preserves using local produce. To mark St Tryphon's Day, the long table inside was set for fellow wine makers, friends and staff. Some twenty people crowded in, helping themselves to bowls of soup with lamb meatballs, roasted vegetables and hunks of bread to eat with the pungent local cheese. Sergei, our enthusiastic host, was busy filling up wine glasses and insisting that it wasn't a restaurant, urging everyone to relax as if they were at home. Although there seemed to be an entire table of food, this was not yet the main event. Next came a succession of platters, each with different layers of the traditional Bulgarian dish called *kanapa*, made by covering a massive oven tray with lamb, then adding stuffed cabbage or vine leaves, sausages, and more cuts of lamb, the whole thing a total of seven different dishes all cooked together and then served up separately again. A couple of local tourism officials were among the guests – leading the toasts to the winemakers and food producers who have kept life and work and jobs going, with the kind of generous hospitality you often see only in the hardest of times.

The St Tryphon celebrations were not over yet. The following day, in the nearby village of Novi Troyan, there was time for another family meal around the table of Sergei and Natalia Vodnik. They had been running a food business in Odesa for more than twenty years, but at the start of the full-scale war – when there were genuine fears that Russian attacks might cut off Bessarabia from the rest of Ukraine – they decided to move the contents of their large city food warehouse to their home village, in order to make sure people there did not run out of supplies. With that came a commitment to build a new business in the village making soft cheese and other dairy products, in order to provide much-needed local jobs and pay taxes back into the community.

Inside their home, another long table was laid for a feast cooked by their mother, Valentina. She single handedly produced bowls of preserved tomatoes with greens in a clear tomato broth, shredded cabbage cooked slowly down with rice and sunflower oil, plates of boiled chicken chopped into pieces, platters of lamb stew, more stuffed vine leaves and a huge soft cheese pie called *banitsa*, made up of rolls of filo pastry filled with the cheese and yoghurt, baked together in a large dish and brushed with egg. Jostling for space were jugs of *kompot*, the juice made from poaching different fruits:

grape, and cherry plum. And many jugs of wine.

Of course, the backdrop of Russia's war was never far away. I sat with a woman who had spent decades working as a doctor. Her phone was full of photographs of her uniformed son, who served as a helicopter pilot. At one point during the meal, between the toasts to life and victory, the table fell silent for a while as she stood up to read a poem which she had written for her son back in 2014 as he carried the injured back from the front. She called the poem 'Anxiety'.

Later that evening, rumbling along the road back towards Odesa, towards the checkpoints and the gridlocked lines of freight lorries with their precious cargo of food, my friend Sasha and I drove past the local cemetery; there were three fresh graves of fallen defenders, three more Ukrainian flags flying their blue and yellow tribute along the verge – the all too familiar drive-by skyline of wartime Ukraine.

Chapter Seventeen

COOKING UNDER OCCUPATION & IN EXILE

When Katrya Kalyuzhna fled from her occupied home town in April 2022, she and her husband packed the car with their most precious possessions. They had room for two families to escape with them, along with her two cats, a few clothes and the sourdough starter she had been baking with for years. Katrya had been working from her home in Kakhovka, a small city of around 30,000 people on the left bank of the Dnipro river in Kherson region. She baked sourdough bread, buns and special cakes like Easter *paska* and *zavyvanets*, a braided loaf filled with a paste made of sweet poppy seed. One of her recipes, for her grandmother's southern borsch, had been published in a book about Ukrainian food and culture. But that normal, happy life was completely torn apart that February, when Russian forces invaded Ukraine, storming through the southern region where she lived. It had been her greatest fear, ever since the Russians annexed Crimea in 2014.

From the moment she heard the first explosions on the outskirts of her home town and saw the endless line of armoured personnel carriers along the bypass, she could barely sleep, and barely breathe. Within a few days, essential produce began to disappear from the shelves. Shops closed down altogether; there was no flour anywhere, and it was impossible to find yeast. Everyone needed bread, she remembers, but there was nowhere to get it, and no way to make it at home. She was contacted by a local old people's home, which had a small bakery on the premises. They still had a small supply of flour, but no yeast, and they knew that Katrya was experienced in making bread using sourdough. For two weeks, until their supplies of flour ran out, she baked bread for the residents, as well as a nearby kindergarten and a hospital.

Even worse than the scarcity of basic food, however, was the emotional trauma. Katrya couldn't talk about it for a long time, although months later, she described the ordeal to the First Western television channel. Imagine that your home, all the places you love, your whole town, is suddenly your prison, she told them. There were collaborators everywhere who could report you at any time. They heard stories of people being arrested in their homes at four o'clock in the morning and taken away. You could be killed, or beaten up, and there would be no one to stop it.

After forty-three days she'd endured enough, even though leaving the occupied territory was highly dangerous. Katrya knew that some of the people who fled in the first few weeks had been shot in their cars. But the Russians finally agreed to set up humanitarian corridors, although they were not that humanitarian, she told me, because the Russian soldiers could open fire at any time. She said the occupiers wanted to get rid of those who hated them, later taking over the empty flats and houses for themselves. But it did at least offer a brief window of opportunity to the thousands of people who wanted to flee into unoccupied Ukraine. She tried to persuade her parents to come with them, as her father was ill, with Parkinson's disease. Her parents insisted on staying: we are old, they said, no one will do anything to us. So Katrya and her husband left them reluctantly behind and began the terrifying journey out of Russian-controlled territory. 'It was twelve hours of horror, rage, danger and fatigue,' she says. 'We went through so many Russian checkpoints, under all their questioning and other disgusting things.' The dirty faces of the soldiers, she says, were imprinted in her memory. As they drove through the grey zone, the area separating occupied territory from free Ukraine, 'we heard the sound of artillery shelling, it was endless.' Finally, they made it through. She describes the smell of occupation as a mixture of adrenaline and fear. But in Mykolaiv, she says, 'We breathed the air of freedom.'

It took a while to settle down in Lviv, the largest city in western Ukraine, with a grand historic centre just forty miles from the Polish border, lined with cafes and chocolate shops. But no matter how beautiful and relatively peaceful, it was a place where nothing was familiar. Then, a few weeks after they'd arrived, Katrya's father died; she was unable to be at his funeral. The grief numbed her for a while, but one day she remembered her sourdough starter, the one she'd brought with her from Kakhovka. She slowly brought it back to life, and made a simple loaf of sourdough bread. She called it her 'bread in exile' and realised that the act of baking was healing, and a way back into daily life. She reached out to a Lviv baker called Vasylyna, whom she had met virtually, on social media. They hit it off immediately, and Katrya began working with Vasylyna in her small micro bakery in an apartment block on the edge of the city, where they baked all kinds of bread, from large sourdough loaves to croissants and sweet buns. One of their specialties was rye bread, which was less familiar to Katrya because no one grew rye in the warmer climate in southern Ukraine.

Work at the bakery helped her to make Lviv into her second home. 'I am more than a thousand kilometres away from home and I have no idea when I will be able to return there. So, I can't just waste time and sit and wait until it happens.' Vasylyna was eager to embrace her local southern Ukrainian recipes and learn from them too. 'I cooked my borsch for Vasylyna and her neighbours, and talked to them about my land, the nature there and the cooking techniques. They were amazed because my Kherson borsch was so different from the one you usually find in Lviv, it was exciting to show them!' She scoured the local markets and talked to stallholders, trying new varieties of fruit, vegetables and beans. 'I found all of them tasted stunning and it inspired me to try new experiments in the kitchen. When we started to prepare for winter I managed to recreate some of my Kherson dishes, but I also learned some new recipes which Vasylyna and her mother showed me. It has become a constant interaction which keeps enriching both of us.'

Katrya had grown up learning to cook from her mother and grandmother, whom she had been named after. 'Her borsch was a true gastronomic icon, it was the most fragrant and delicious I had ever tasted. It became the first thing I really wanted to cook after mastering some easy dishes. Once she had given me the step-by-step recipe I managed to cook it confidently a few months later.' She had given up eating meat in her teens and learned how to preserve and pickle all sorts of vegetables and herbs. 'We never bought sauerkraut, pickles or jam from a shop. Everything on our table came from our own cellar, the same as most Ukrainians who come from the countryside.' At home she had cooked simple vegetable dishes: buckwheat with mushrooms, rice with spice and herbs. They made their own curd cheese and sour cream. As well as bread, she learned how to make enriched dough and desserts for special family occasions. All her familiar dishes sprang from the land and the produce around Kherson. 'They call it the region of four seas: the Sea of Azov, the Black Sea, the Kakhovka Sea, which is the reservoir in the Dnipro river, and the endless seas of wheat fields.' It meant that bread, as well as fish, was a part of their everyday diet. 'I can't forget the local fishmongers, all those baskets of flounder, carp, pike and freshly caught prawns. My favourite break was to walk along the Azov shore, to breathe the fresh, salty air. It has become a cherished dream.'

I have been to visit Katrya at Vasylyna's bakery in Lviv many times over the last two and a half years, usually in the middle of the day when Katrya is making their staff lunch, and there is always a new cake or loaf of bread to try. I have made dozens of Katrya's recipes at home in London, but it is always so much better when she can show me herself, with masterclasses on how to make 'no-knead' bread, pizzas and *varenyky* dumplings filled with raisins and curd cheese.

On my last visit Katrya had decided to make the fat, coiled-up pies called *vertuta*, stretching each sheet of filo-type pastry across a table until it was impossibly thin. She filled one with a mixture of caramelised onion, cabbage and potato, while the other one had rose petal and strawberry jam with crushed walnuts, rather like one I had tried in Bessarabia. As they came out of the oven, she sliced them into quarters and we tried a piece of each, barely waiting for it to cool down. Like all Katrya's food, they were incredibly delicious.

In the jars carefully stacked onto a small shelf, there are home-made pickles and jams, and special mixtures of spices and herbs. She has experimented with making za'atar, offering a pinch for me to try, and asked if it has too much salt. We tasted some thickened plum compote called *kysil*, which she made to go with the sweet *varenyky*. There is always a vegetable soup on the stove, sometimes her grandmother's borsch, or a summer version with lemony sorrel and dill. And huge, thick slices of cake, sometimes a layered one with chocolate and plum jam, or a sourdough honey cake with a damp crumb and a slightly fermented flavour, perfect with a spoonful or two of sour cream.

Katrya managed to get her mother out of Kakhovka eventually, on an even more traumatic evacuation journey. The Russians would only allow a few cars through their checkpoints every hour, leaving people stuck in the blazing heat of summer, waiting to pass through, for five days. Her mother is now in Lviv, along with her sister and her family, and she has her cats, so the city is no longer full of strangers. Although she still dreams of the day when she will be able to return home, Kakhovka is not the bright, carefree place of her childhood. Her memories are darkened by the trauma of the occupation which they fled, the air which smelled of desperation and fear. By the beginning of 2024, Ukrainian prosecutors were looking into more than 21,000 alleged crimes against civilians in the occupied Kherson region. Their investigations included murders, attacks on civilians and illegal imprisonment carried out both by Russian forces and the occupation authorities. Katrya, who still has relatives living under these conditions, has managed to hold on to one dream. 'I am a baker, and I will go on baking my Ukrainian bread, and no Russian will stop me,' she says.

Across Lviv, I went to meet Lerane Khaybullayeva, who's been forced to move home not once, but four times. She was from Crimea, the peninsula on the north coast of the Black Sea which was illegally annexed by Russia in 2014. Under Stalin, the entire Tatar population had been deported en masse to the Urals and Central Asia, and banned from returning to their homeland. Lerane's family were among them, and she had been born in exile in Uzbekistan. After the collapse of the old USSR in the early 1990s, they had managed to return to Crimea. She was eight years old at the time, and her family were starting life all over again. Just before we met, I had watched an interview she gave to the TV station Current Time. She had described a bus trip with her grandmother to her home town, her father planting huge crops of apples, cherries and raspberries, swimming in the north Crimean canal and reading books on the beach. She felt truly Crimean, she told them, when she began reading poems by the Tatar writer Lili Budzhorova. 'Of what does the motherland smell? Of a dry blade of grass, caught in a child's hair...' She became a journalist, a successful one, but after Russian troops marched into the peninsula in 2014, leading an overtly Ukrainian life became incredibly risky. After two years under occupation, Lerane decided to leave, moving to the leafy town of Irpin near Kyiv where she wanted to preserve her family's recipes and traditions. 'I had always worked as a journalist,' she told me, 'but in Kyiv I wanted to have a place where I could tell stories of Crimea every day. The real history, the past, the present and the future.'

She opened a small cafe called Crimean Yard, but that too fell victim to Russia's war. In the early days of the full-scale invasion, Irpin came under heavy shelling as Russian warplanes flew overhead: homes, shops and bridges were destroyed and Lerane and her young family were forced to flee their home yet again. 'When I saw Russian tanks there, I felt the same as I had felt in Crimea. I had my son to take care of, he was only ten. We had to leave.' Her husband joined the armed forces, and Lerane ended up in Lviv, where she managed to open another Crimean Yard in September 2023. It is a pretty place, in one of the narrow cobbled streets in the historic centre of the city, and we chatted over cups of strong, sweet coffee. 'I took these cups with me when we left – they were made in Turkey but I took them from my parents' house in Crimea. They are a memory of my home. It's always black coffee, without milk, and you should drink it with a little dessert.'

The small dining room was bedecked with photographs and memorabilia from Crimea, with a large map of the peninsula on one wall, dating back to 1935. 'I decided a small cafe was the best way to introduce people to Crimea,' she said. 'A place where we could prepare our national dishes, like *chiyberek*.' Before starting the cafe, she had never cooked professionally, but she decided to start with her grandmother's recipe for *chiyberek*, a flat pastry filled with a savoury mince meat mixture and deep-fried until crisp. 'That's how it all started,' she said. 'Cooking and eating food, listening to music and talking over a meal is a really good way to pass on information,' she said. 'There is so much fake news out there, on the internet and in newspapers. I wanted to give people a first-hand account of how we lived in Crimea, from my own experience, so that people would understand that it was completely genuine and not fake.' By making the dishes from her heritage, she said she could tell stories about her family and what had happened to them. 'And then people will be more likely to believe it and remember it, because it is taken from our real life.'

Chiyberek, which you can find in fast-food outlets around Ukraine, remains Crimea's most famous dish, and is often called *cheburek* – although Lerane insisted it should be pronounced differently. 'It is more like "chiy-burek".' She said it had been recognised by UNESCO on the list of

Ukraine's intangible cultural heritage, with the chance that it would be protected still further – rather like how the chef Yevhen Klopotenko managed for Ukrainian borsch. At the cafe, she preferred to make a slightly healthier stuffed flatbread called *yantiq*, a thin bread folded around various different fillings, which is baked rather than fried.

'We also make Uzbek-style dishes here, because the Crimean people were deported there in 1944, and they began taking on some of the dishes they saw there. So now things like *plov* have become part of the Crimean Tatar repertoire.' I asked if it was hard to find specific ingredients. 'Ukraine and Crimea are all one country, so we share all the key ingredients: onions, potatoes, all the vegetables. We have the best-tasting produce here, our seeds and crops are popular across the world!' She wanted me to try some sweets with the coffee, and fetched over some bowls of fried pastry, glistening in syrup. 'This is *pakhlava*. It is one of our traditional desserts, perhaps the most famous. You must try it. We also prepare rose petal jam, and another jam made with figs.' The *pakhlava* was incredibly light and crisp, and despite the pools of syrup dripping off the shards of pastry, somehow managed not to be overwhelmingly sweet. 'We make almost everything in-house, except this *pakhlava*. It's baked by a Crimean lady who was living in Kherson, and now she lives near Lviv. She has five children and her husband is in the army. But she can bake this, and we buy it, and it helps to keep her family going.' The Turkish coffee, she said, was one of the few overseas products she uses, although she made the drink the Crimean way, but on a more modern gas stove rather than a hearth. 'Turkey has a big shared history with Crimea – we are all part of the Black Sea region along with Greece and Bulgaria, so we have many similarities.'

Dessert finished, Lerane showed us around the space she calls her 'museum of memories'. 'They are all different memories of Crimea, gifts from Tatar people, or Ukrainians who visited before Russian occupation; everything on display has a big story behind it.' She pointed to some pebbles encased in a small picture frame. 'These are stones from a beach near Sevastopol. It was a gift from someone who lived there and saved this piece of land.' There was a series of prints, depicting native Crimean herbs and plants. 'I see this as a kind of cultural diplomacy, but through food,' she said. 'I often sit here in the cafe, and when customers come in we talk a lot about Crimea. Food allows you to really help people understand things about their own history and life, how Crimea is part of Ukraine. Many people, especially young people, have never been able to visit because of occupation, but at least they can experience some of Crimea's culture here.'

The atmosphere in this cafe, she said, was completely different from her time in Kyiv, before the full-scale war. 'There were never that many young customers in Irpin; it was older people who just wanted to sit and eat the food. But here in Lviv, lots of youth come in and they are really interested in our history. So that's why I often sit here and tell stories to anyone who wants to listen. It is so important for the future of Ukraine, to know all of our history.' A shelf was crammed with Crimean books: some stories in Ukrainian translated from the Tatar language, and some popular Ukrainian poets translated into Tatar. There were language-lesson books for children. The 1935 map on the wall had place names written in the Tatar language. 'People can see how it used to be written, the old names of places which were changed under the Russian empress Catherine II or later, in Soviet times. The map was given to us by a lady who escaped from Crimea. Her grandfather had been in the

Soviet army, and this map came from those times. We have it in pride of place because it is so important.' She described her relationship with the community in Lviv as a kind of collective therapy session.

Some more desserts arrived, and Lerane talked me through some of the recipes. 'To make this *pakhlava* you must roll out the dough really thin. You cut it into strips and make a lot of layers, then take small pieces and fry it, and serve it just like this, with honey or syrup and crushed nuts. It should be crisp and not heavy, not too sweet.' There are similar desserts, she said, in places like Azerbaijan, Turkistan and beyond. 'It is the Slavic world. Many nationalities. Crimean Tatars are part of this family.' The Tatar kitchen, she says, is not complicated. 'Most of our spices come from the Uzbek and Turkish traditions, and we make things which are easy to cook. I can only think of one dish we make with fish. Maybe it's because everyone was deported to Uzbekistan all those years ago, and the older recipes were lost. The Soviets destroyed all of our gastronomic and culinary treasure.'

A large group of people had come in, and Lerane went over to chat; one of them was a Crimean illustrator and she brought me a catalogue of his work, signed inside the front cover as a gift. Later that night, she said, they would be holding a music event. 'I translate the music for my guests, because it's another way to experience and remember Crimea. I don't want them just to come here for the food, but also to really feel as if they were at home.' Of course, all she wanted was to go back to her own home in Crimea, that magical place with its beaches and coves and orchards filled with fruit. 'I won't open a Crimean cafe there, but a Ukrainian one, because for ten years people there forgot what it was like to be part of Ukraine. And it will be time to begin creating a new story in Crimea, a Ukrainian story.'

Chapter Eighteen

BRIGHT YOUNG CHEFS

Odesa is a magical city, cradled by the dark, glittering waters of the Black Sea. The historic centre is lined with the grandeur of UNESCO-protected architecture, while everywhere you can see a riot of cultures and traditions. To be in Odesa is to love life. My friend Maria, who was writing a book about Odesan food, had first opened my eyes to its unique culinary heritage in the late summer of 2022. It was a happy and vibrant mix of Jewish, Ukrainian, Romanian, Greek, Italian and Russian influences. The local food markets were overflowing with incredible seasonal produce: ripe lush tomatoes, sweet cherries and strawberries, tiny new potatoes and bright bunches of herbs. Most of one room was devoted to different kinds of cream and curd cheese, including a unique version made with the baked milk called *ryazhenka*. And it was also a city where some of the country's brightest young chefs were producing exciting, modern Ukrainian food, which paid respect to the past but was emphatically not your grandmother's cooking.

Nika Lozovska's restaurant, Dizyngoff, is right in the centre of Odesa, overlooking the famous Potemkin Steps, which lead right down to the port. During the first months of war, that precarious time when it seemed that the Russians might try to invade Odesa by sea, the area was completely shut down, ringed by tank traps, the majestic view hidden behind a wall of sandbags bristling with machine-gun positions. When I first visited in September 2022, the city centre was still in the process of opening up.

Even as the businesses around Katerynynska Square began getting back to some kind of normality, all that military paraphernalia was still an intimidating sight, although everyone was grateful for those who were keeping the city safe. 'We had to close for around five or six months after the full-scale war began, because the city centre was blocked. They would only allow people who live here to enter,' Nika told me. 'But then at the end of July they managed to agree a new grain deal. The day it was agreed, two huge Kaliber rockets landed here at the port, as if the Russians wanted to show that they didn't care about the agreement they had just signed. It was so loud here at the restaurant because we overlooked the port. But that was the very day that we reopened and began to work. And then there was the crazy winter that year with no electricity, and the same again now. But it has all made us so much stronger.'

We were sitting at my favourite table, the small one by the front window, with a view over the now renamed 'European Square'. A statue of the Russian empress Catherine was torn down in the winter of 2022, and replaced by a Ukrainian flag. Nika, impeccably dressed in her chef's jacket, her terrier Hugo running around her feet, organised some food: Dizyngoff's speciality, salted anchovy served simply with *labneh* cheese on fresh black rye bread. 'Our biggest challenge was that first winter without electricity,' she said. The city authorities had tried to organise schedules, to let people know when their power was likely to be on, but in practice, nothing worked. 'Odesa region was the most badly damaged of all, so most of the time we had no electricity at all. We had no funds to buy our own generator, and although we managed to raise some money we really hesitated to spend it, because we hardly had any guests. Even if we bought the generator, we didn't know how we could afford fuel for it. We were short on money and short on guests, but somehow we managed to hang on until the following spring and then it all got a bit easier. The power cuts ended and people began coming back to Odesa and we had got through the most difficult times.'

Nika had built up an enthusiastic and loyal following in the nine years Dizyngoff had been open. It hadn't been easy, opening a place which proudly championed modern Ukrainian food, at a time when people often expected foreign ingredients and dishes which their families didn't cook at home. 'We had what you might call an inferiority complex, that our own Ukrainian food should always cost less than foreign food. Whereas in France, for example, people really appreciate what is French, and it's absolutely number one for them. Here this concept has only recently begun to take off, so we have always tried to compensate with our creativity. We don't just do the basic Ukrainian dishes, we change them, we change techniques, we make them lighter and more modern. It's a constant process of invention.'

The Covid pandemic, she said, first made them appreciate the importance of local produce. 'Then we realised that it wasn't just during those times that it was more logical. It is always fresher, it is always tastier, it just makes more sense. I'm a locavore myself; whenever I travel somewhere I want to eat things which are local to that place. So somehow it became part of our identity.' The team created some special dishes that have been on the menu since the start. 'We serve sea snails called *rapani*, they have become a signature dish, we just change up the garnish according to the season. They have a reputation for being a bit chewy, but we are the only place to cook and serve them whole. We have found the perfect cooking time and temperature to make them melt in the mouth. In spring, we will make them with wild garlic, you can already see it on sale in the markets – I like to call it the first sign of spring.' I asked about the anchovies on toast, which had become famous ever since Nika appeared in a documentary about Odesa food, made by the popular Ukrainian food bloggers Anton Ptushkin and Misha Katsurin. 'We use bread from our friends at DOU bakery, their dark rye. We make our own *labneh* cheese, and we salt the anchovies. That's all they need, just salt and time. They taste a little like sashimi and we make them every day so the dish is really fresh. It doesn't need any super-crazy modern technique, just great bread and butter and always super-fresh fish. I have a feeling that nowadays, during the war, people feel like eating things which aren't over-complicated.'

Over the years, she's built up a network of trusted suppliers all over the region and beyond. Sometimes they come into the restaurant, carrying boxes of wild mushrooms picked in the forests nearby, or trays of fish from the Black Sea. 'Just the other day I had a message from one of our suppliers from a place called Bila Tserkva, near Kyiv. He sells beautiful asparagus. He's actually serving in the army now, but his parents are taking care of his business. He was checking in, to see if we are still ordering this year, what we are planning.' With his produce, Dizyngoff came up with an ambitious asparagus menu to mark the season, including a take on the anchovy dish, serving lightly grilled asparagus and *labneh* on toasted black rye, with a wild garlic oil and a salted lemon relish. Asparagus also became the seasonal accompaniment to the *rapani* sea snails, along with tiny new potatoes and plenty of herbs. Nika ran through a list of other suppliers who had been even more affected by the war.

'We used to buy cider from one guy, he made really amazing cider, but then his production place was shelled. We had another supplier who was next to Kherson, and his place was occupied.' It is a constant litany of memories and loss.

When the restaurant first reopened back in the summer of '22, Nika decided to create some special dishes to raise money for the armed forces. She put borsch on the menu for the first time, and *varenyky* dumplings filled with potato. 'The borsch is a mixture of different family recipes. Somehow both my mother's and father's sides of the family made it without meat, so here at Dizyngoff we make a vegetarian base. A lot of people really appreciate it, and you will never notice that it doesn't have a broth made from beef. Maybe it's because we are a Jewish family and we wanted to serve it with sour cream, or perhaps it was about not having enough money for expensive meat. My grandmother and my mum don't even fry the vegetables, which is one of the most traditional ways of making it. They would just cut everything up and make sure they put a lot of vegetables in, and it was always really good. So that's how we make our borsch here.'

Inside the city itself, Odesa's fresh food markets have remained a source of inspiration throughout the year. 'Together with Alexander, who is my head chef, we brainstorm together and get inspired by the farmers and the produce. I often go on a search for the most interesting cheeses, new varieties of potatoes, tomatoes, and zucchini flowers. We use a lot of the wild sea asparagus or glasswort, which grows around an hour's drive from here, so we go and pick it ourselves. The recipes are somehow born very naturally.' Like a lot of energetic young chefs, they sought out people to learn from and collaborate with. 'We invite each other for pop-ups, or for charity dinners. We created one event together called *Probudzhennya*, which means

'Awakening'. It was to symbolise our awakening to the new reality, where we all have to work to support the army, but by doing things we love, with a great energy together.' She relies on a group of friends who all share the same cooking philosophy. 'We have the same vibe, we have this mission to create recipes which we are proud of, with Ukrainian produce, and are on the same level as any other European city. It's even cool to see how this horrible situation brought us all together.' We talked about a collaborative dinner which she had recently put together with four other chefs from Lviv, Kyiv and Odesa. 'They came up with six dishes and Dizyngoff created three, and we put on two dinners. One was a kind of trial run, and we invited our friends along, including some who have been serving in the army. The next day we did it for real, with a lot more guests, and it was an amazing event with an art auction on the side. We raised something like $20,000 and it was all for charity. Everyone was so happy to work on it for free; the artists donated their work, so we collected this incredible amount. People had been missing this kind of event too, getting all dressed up for a special night.'

It was early evening by the time we finished talking, a plate of *syrniki* curd cheese pancakes on a pool of thick cream, festooned with caramelised nuts and berries, almost finished on the table between us. The restaurant was starting to fill up again, mostly tables of young women, or older couples. Nika's dog Hugo stood at attention beside the door, as if he was checking the credentials of the guests stepping inside. 'The way I see it,' Nika said, 'a restaurant is a place where you can get the feeling of the way it was before, and the way it will be again after the war. There is a chance for a moment to forget life, where you go to treat yourself. To regain a calmer state of mind.'

Hundreds of miles east, in Kharkiv, I went to meet Nika's friend Mykyta Virchenko. Barely twenty-seven, he had already made a name for himself with his restaurant Tripichya, which he opened in the spring of 2023 in a building which had once been a parish school. It's the restaurant everyone will tell you to go to as soon as you mention Kharkiv: 'Have you been to Tripichya? You must go!'

Mykyta, a slight young man with an intense gaze and a shock of curly hair, has the kind of boundless energy which might be explained by the fact that he began his working life in specialist coffee. He joined a company called Sweeter and became the brand manager, taking charge of around a hundred employees in twenty-five shops. He loved the science behind it, and developed a signature drink to enter into competitions. He wanted to build a factory and make it into a business. 'I thought this is our chance, we can make some really great Ukrainian drinks, which would be really high quality. But they said they didn't have the money or the vision for it.' So he set up on his own, creating his own vinegar made from spiced rum, which he used in his lemonades. 'This vinegar had such a special quality. When you drink a lemonade made from lemons or oranges, you feel a kind of freshness, and some acidity on your tongue. But when you try the one made with this vinegar, it had such an intense acidity – you just feel it there, it is so complex, almost radiant.' He was almost fizzing himself with the excitement of describing it. He felt it was one of the most important things he had done. But then, that summer, on a holiday in the Carpathian mountains, a revelation suddenly came to him: he wanted to cook food.

With no background in cooking, he started at the bottom, contacting a chef called Ivan Shishkin, who long before the war, had cooked at a well-regarded Moscow restaurant called

Delicatessen. Shishkin had gone on to collaborate with restaurant entrepreneur Alex Cooper to open the Odesa Food Market. 'So I went to Odesa and said to Shishkin, let's work together. I was there for two or three months, not even being paid, and he hardly spoke to me. I had come from this job where I had hundreds of employees and all of a sudden I was in this kitchen as an assistant, and I was thinking what the fuck, it's another world, I am hating this. It was the worst time of my life.' But he persevered. 'Every day I was in this fish restaurant, trying to make something which would make Shishkin look at me and take notice. And after about two months they finally gave me my first project.' Cooper was about to open a new Israeli-style restaurant called Shalom, and Mykyta was given the task of developing a Yemeni bread called *malawach* for the menu. 'I was making this *malawach* all the time for about two weeks; I made ten different types of dough, and tried all the different kinds of oil, butter and salt. Every day I went around the food market and gave pieces of this bread to chefs who work there so they could tell me what they thought. And finally I understood that I had made a good *malawach*, it was glossy with lots of layers and you could pull it apart when it was baked. I gave some to Shishkin, and he said, "Yeah, it's OK," but he finally saw that I could be trusted with more challenging work and that I would think only about the process until I understood it entirely. He started to give me more things to do, and stayed with me for one hour, then two, until we were working together, talking about all kinds of things, and at the time I thought that Ivan Shishkin was maybe the best chef that ever came to Ukraine. He was educated in chemistry and biology, which is so crucial for chefs, and had a really important vision for his food.'

With just six months mentoring he had acquired the kind of knowledge and experience which might have taken ten years. He came back to Kharkiv eager to open his own restaurant, and had plans for an Asian-style bistro with ramen and a specialist sake bar. 'I thought to myself, I will be so ready. And then all this crazy stuff started.' The crazy stuff was the full-scale Russian invasion, and Kharkiv was right on the front line. Mykyta's family had a meeting to work out what to do. They only had a small car, his elderly grandfather was unwell, and the roads were clogged with people trying to escape. 'We stayed underground for a few days, because the city was really like hell, and then on the fourth day my friend wrote to me and said they needed help taking some chicken to a volunteer kitchen because it was so important to feed people. So I'm with my mum, we have our little Toyota, and we drove to this factory, there were missiles coming, it was all panic, but we managed to find the guys with the chicken and they just threw it in the back of the car, half frozen.' It was like being plunged into the middle of a dystopian film.

'We had this car full of raw chicken which was defrosting around our feet, driving through the city, and out of the window we see flames, burned-out cars, people running from fire, it really was like hell.' They made it to the volunteer kitchen which had been set up in the city's zoo, where they told him they didn't have enough hands to do all the cooking. He ended up volunteering there for three months. 'It was certainly an interesting time of my life. We were cooking around 150 portions a day, and then we started growing. It became not so much a kitchen, more of a factory, where we made four tonnes of food a week for one of the army battalions – we made three portions of food every day for each of them.' Their priority, he said, was hygiene and food safety, so that no one would get sick. He was especially proud of their borsch. 'It cost only a few hryvnias per portion but it really was gastronomic, it wasn't just a basic borsch. I think working there was one of the best things I ever did in my life. There were all sorts of volunteers, it was bank managers and people from IT, a guy who repairs trains, rappers – so many people and none of them were paid. We just paid the cleaners because they were really doing the hard work.'

After the zoo kitchen, Mykyta wondered if he could revive his dream of opening an Asian bistro, and after finding a central Kharkiv site, they created Tripichya, named for the three ovens they built themselves, each one for a different method of cooking. The local market was close by, and they decided they would just cook food each day, depending on what was for sale. They ditched the Asian concept and set out to do modern Ukrainian food, perfecting every process from scratch.

Some food arrived on the table as we talked, and Mykyta started describing each dish. 'This hummus, it is not the basic kind, it starts with beans which we cook, then we make our own tahini by hand, not using any special equipment. This salad isn't just chopped beetroot, we use lacto-fermentation which takes a lot of time, it is our version of the beetroot salad made with vinegar which everyone has at home.' He picked up a small plate of *varenyky*. 'These dumplings, we make the dough, we fill them with our home-made cheese, and the sauce is made with browned butter and carrot juice. You have to wash the carrots and peel them, to filter the liquid. You have to cook the butter down until it has this nutty smell from the roasted milk. You emulsify the two together. Just think about the amount of time it takes to make these two dumplings, and how many people are involved in the process.'

The very last thing he wanted was to make comfort food: 'I understand it,' he said, 'but this is not my story.' Instead he wanted to challenge people, and make them learn about what they were consuming, like the coffee specialists he had worked with before. After coming to Tripichya a few times, he said, customers would know the difference between cuts of meat, how it tastes and where it comes from. 'A lot of people are talking about Ukrainian food, but to me it's about the ingredients and the terroir, and rooting it in a specific place. We know it's something we have to be proud of. It's not just our grandmothers' recipes, but also when you go to the market here every day and you see these tomatoes or this sunflower seed or this beetroot, which are all incredible, you can see the quality. And it's all from local farms in the Kharkiv region.' He was forming plans to open a place inside the market, which would be run by one of his chefs, as well as a baker. 'You would just go into the market, grab something fresh, this product that was a few hours ago still in the ground, and you'll just make some kind of street food and sell it right away. You work seven hours, when the market is open. It's the kind of thing people want now, we have such good ingredients and I just want to respect that.'

He was busy organising a special event for the following month with his former chef Ilya, who was getting one day off in Kharkiv to cook a fundraising dinner so they could buy a truck for his artillery unit.

The special event took place a few weeks later, a night on which everything was cooked over fire. The restaurant was filled with people sitting in semi-darkness, happily tearing into charred flatbreads and sharing plates of extraordinary food. For Ilya, back in civilian clothes and with his friends in the kitchen again for a night, it was pure joy. Working at Tripichya, he said, had made him feel at home for the first time in twelve years as a chef. 'When I came back here, I had that same feeling again, especially after being in the army when you are in a completely different, and very stressful environment. And especially feeding people who know you, love you and respect you. It's pure happiness!'

To Yevhen Klopotenko, who has become Ukraine's closest thing to a celebrity chef, the drive to promote Ukrainian cuisine to the rest of the world is an essential part of national diplomacy. At his Kyiv restaurant 100 Rokiv Tomu Vpered, which roughly translates as '100 years ago in the future', he was dressed in a chef's jacket and a pair of shorts. Just a few days earlier he had hosted the US Secretary of State Antony Blinken and his entourage for lunch, telling them that from now on, their life would be divided into two: 'Before you taste borsch, and after.' If you want to present your country to others, he said, you can do it through food. 'It helps people understand on a really fundamental level, in their DNA, what this nation is really about. When I realised that the Russians want to take everything from us, even the food, I started to think that if invaders want to take our food, it means that it is something really important.' Klopotenko had been instrumental in persuading UNESCO to declare borsch to be part of Ukraine's national heritage, and he wanted that to become the first step in a global journey. 'First you get borsch recognised by UNESCO. Then someone opens a Ukrainian restaurant. The restaurant gets on to some prestigious list, and everyone writes about it. Then someone goes there and decides to open a chain of places with Ukrainian cuisine, and step by step it will spread all around the world, and people will discover Ukraine through our gastronomy. You might be sitting in America, you can't travel here but you can go to a restaurant, try the food and end up understanding something about this nation. That's how it works, and it is a very powerful instrument.'

This kind of journey into self-expression, he said, was happening across culture: in music, in art, even politics. 'Everything was organised according to the old rules, but now we are trying to make our new Ukrainian rules.' Now the challenge lay in trying to find the right balance between respecting tradition and modernity. I mentioned a piece in the *New York Times* – 'Everything Old Is New Again', about the growing trend for nostalgia. 'I think sometimes people in the West are looking to the past as some kind of haven of authenticity. Here it's very different. We are not looking for our identity; we are building on it, something for the next fifty years.'

A connection to the land, and the food which grows there, is clearly part of that identity. For decades, during Soviet times, no one trusted the government, and they preferred to buy from farmers' markets rather than shops. Most people grew their own food, and learned how to preserve it. 'It's a Ukrainian tradition that every few weeks your mother or your grandmother who lives in the village would send you fruit and vegetables. No one ever asked if you needed them or not, it was like a mindset, a rule which must be followed.' His mother had recently visited him, and brought about ten kilograms of cucumbers with her. There were so many cucumbers that he brought huge bags of them into the restaurant to share among the staff. 'It's in our DNA to grow food. My mother knows she could grow twenty-five times less, but she wants to be sure she has enough.'

It's a trait which stood many people in good stead when the full-scale invasion happened. 'I think in England if every shop suddenly closed down overnight, there would be a big panic, it would be a catastrophe. Here, when all the shops and businesses closed down, everyone said, "No worries, we have everything from our gardens." Food isn't some kind of luxury here, it is more fundamental, because the memory of being without it is still very immediate.' And, of course, the unity that sprang from confronting their violent neighbour across the border. 'That's also in our DNA. We are living near Russia all our lives, and so in our brains there is resistance, resistance. If you are together, you can do whatever you want. When we see the enemy so clearly, we can be united. If you need me to help, I will help. If you need me to cook, I will cook. It's about survival, and the most basic instinct to keep living.'

So, in Odesa, the food market is full of traders, and elderly ladies who come by bus from nearby villages clutching plastic bags of herbs and tiny potatoes, berries and extravagant flowers. Nika will visit, basket in hand, to pick up the best-looking mushrooms, perfect tomatoes, sweet juicy plums. In Kharkiv, despite the darkness of blackouts and the constant threat of Russian glide bombs, Tripichya manages to host a special dinner, with a chef who now cooks for an artillery unit on the front lines, and they will raise money he needs to buy them a truck. And still, in these dishes, and this Ukrainian produce, they manage to find joy.

Chapter Nineteen

LATE NIGHT AT THE
DE-OCCUPIED SAUNA

The very last thing I expected to do in Izyum was go to a late-night sauna. In the car on the way back from a dystopian bombed-out city on the edge of the front line, Vlad Malashchenko had been letting off steam. 'We should celebrate this day, that we are still alive,' he declared, yanking the steering wheel alarmingly as the car slalomed its way around the jagged chasms of Donetsk region's fractured roads. 'Let's go to the sauna!'

I thought he was joking; as if there would be any such thing in Izyum, a half-destroyed town which had been left shattered by the long months of violent Russian occupation and Ukraine's determined battle to seize it back.

It was already nine when we pulled up in front of a darkened building which looked like it had been abandoned for a long time. Inside the entrance was a sort of kiosk, selling lurid-coloured beers which you could get decanted into your own plastic pop bottle, and an assortment of dried fish and salted nuts. Behind the beer kiosk was a secret door which opened onto a small supermarket, where the volunteers quickly filled a trolley with several bottles of vodka, mineral water, Fanta and some large bags of crisps. Snack time at the de-occupied sauna.

As well as Vlad, there was his friend and driver Yuri, a veteran Japanese newspaper correspondent, and our host, a wiry man in his early sixties who everyone called Yurich, strong enough to repeatedly lift a sixteen-kilogram kettlebell high above his head with one arm. Yurich had become something of a local hero in Izyum: he had sheltered sixty-five people, five dogs and numerous cats in his basement for several months, during the worst of the vicious fighting. The youngest was a three-month-old baby, his goddaughter; the oldest, a lady of almost ninety. There was no electricity, no heating, no light, and just one outside toilet between them. For three weeks, during the very worst time, when the shelling barely stopped, even for a second, there was a constant twenty-four-hour curfew: it was impossible for anyone to go outside at all. They searched for food in the rubble of destroyed buildings, made candles out of potatoes. Yurich grabbed a bottle and poked it underneath his shirt to show us how they had managed to survive. 'This is the way we tried to warm up water to make porridge for the children.'

A year and a half after Izyum was liberated by the armed forces of Ukraine, the lights now shine brightly in Yurich's basement; there is a large flat-screen television screwed to the wall, playing the non-stop wartime news channel United Marathon. The other walls are festooned with religious pictures, Ukrainian flags, even a few cartoons. Several dogs are wandering around, while a cat, as cats do, has commandeered the only warm spot in the place, on an old office chair next to the wood-fired stove. The Japanese correspondent has somehow been persuaded to make Asian food for dinner, chopping up pieces of pork, cabbage and chilli and pushing them around a pan over the ancient stove, which is giving off only the faintest glow of heat. He stabs at the stir-fry experiment with a spoon, before abandoning it to carry on cooking while we are out. I am unsure how successful this strategy will be, but it is in keeping with the surreal nature of the entire evening.

We pile into Yurich's car and drive through deserted streets before pulling up outside another building which looks completely closed. This, it turns out, is the sauna. We get changed in the narrow cloakroom; I have insisted on everyone wearing towels, selecting possibly the world's largest bath sheet for myself, and we pad through into a small room where a TV set is inexplicably showing a 1970s Eurovision Song Contest, along with a table that is soon covered with our supermarket sweep selection of Fanta, vodka and snacks. The sauna itself is fierce and hot and smells of eucalyptus; there is a cold plunge pool and a scary-looking bucket thing hanging from a rope which you could use to douse yourself with freezing water, if you were truly insane. Vlad tries it and yells out in shock; I suddenly learn some new Ukrainian swear words. The place is sparkling clean, and after the many hours of bone-chilling cold during our trip around the bleak hellscape of Donetsk oblast, in the heat of the sauna, it is finally warm again. Vlad, recovered from his bucket of freezing water escapade, is making another toast: 'To victory.'

It is eleven o'clock – curfew time in Izyum – when we finally drive back to the basement where the Japanese correspondent's pork and cabbage melange is simmering away in its frying pan. He pokes at it again, adds a liberal dollop of hot sauce and more chilli and spoons it onto some plates. Yurich rifles through a cupboard, pulling out some jars of pickled cucumbers and mixed vegetables for me: '*Domashne* – home-made!' Improbably, the pork stir fry is pronounced a success. 'Normally I don't eat anything spicy,' says Vlad, forking up a large piece of chilli. 'But this is good!'

The United Marathon is showing footage on a loop: a Russian warship in the Black Sea, which has that morning been destroyed by a Ukrainian drone. Two large, elderly dogs, lounging on a bed of blankets in front of the screen, are half dozing, half watching the blurry black and white video of the distant ship going down in a plume of smoke. A good excuse for another toast: Yurich dives back into his cupboard and emerges with a lethal-looking jar of fermented honeycomb in home-brewed alcohol, which looks like something inside is still alive and smells like something died. The guys egg each other on to drink shots of it, and I learn a few more Ukrainian swear words.

It is midnight in Izyum, after this most unlikely of nights at the sauna, in this basement tucked underneath a broken building, all jagged pieces of wood and blackened concrete, with hand-painted letters on the gate still proclaiming 'People Live Here', this basement which once saved the lives of sixty-five residents as rockets slammed into the flats next door, as artillery shells tore through the asphalt; this basement in a city which has lived through the unspeakable horror of occupation, is now a home, quiet and cosy and no longer filled with people huddled together in fear.

And in the morning, on the way to buy a breakfast hot dog and some petrol station coffee, Vlad will take a detour to the Kremyanets hilltop above the city, which he tells me was a local beauty spot where people once went for picnics. We will drive past a bomb-damaged church, past the graffiti on a Second World War monument proclaiming glory to Ukraine and the secret Bansky mural, past the signposts warning of the danger of mines, and at the top, there will be an incredible view, right to Kharkiv and left to Donetsk and Luhansk – sweeping over the city and across the fields beyond. The wind will pick up, for it is almost spring, and it will seem like the whole of Ukraine is there, laid out for all to see below.

AFTERWORD
AND THEN THERE WERE THREE

At the time of writing, Bake for Ukraine now has three mobile bakeries, two of them under repair at a workshop in Odesa. The one in Mykolaiv remains hard at work, turning out sourdough loaves and neat, square rolls under the capable hands of Oleg and Anatoly, a local volunteer. Friends have been delivering the bread to villages in the Mykolaiv and Kherson regions, where it is always happily received. On one trip to a badly damaged village, a woman was so delighted to see some proper Ukrainian *palyanytsya* that she held it to her face for several minutes, smelling and kissing the loaf over and over again.

Winter is approaching, and the first snow has fallen, while the Russian attacks on energy infrastructure are ramping up. One November night, when more than two hundred missiles and drones flew at towns and cities across Ukraine, drones fell on homes in Mykolaiv, killing two women and injuring seven others, the explosion not far from where the bakery is located. In Odesa, power supplies shut down and people were left queueing for water supplies in the street, while a missile armed with cluster munitions slammed into a residential street, leaving at least eight people dead. A friend messaged me, distraught: people are near breaking point, she said. At the same time, Bake for Ukraine managed to locate and deliver a much-needed professional dough mixer for the village near the Belarus border which had donated the two new mobile bakeries. It has already been installed and they are using it to bake for people in need. There is a new initiative in the works to help train injured veterans in baking, so they can learn some skills for a future non-military life.

This is a nervous and uncertain time for Ukraine; the heartbreak of loss is everywhere. But so too is the overwhelming drive to keep helping, and to keep sharing that Ukrainian bread which is almost as precious as gold.

www.bakeforukraine.org

RECIPES

PALYANYTSYA

This recipe for Ukrainian *palyanytsya* bread was created by Katrya Kalyuzhna and Mykola Nevrev for Bake for Ukraine. It's been baked in their mobile bakery and by sourdough bakers all over the world.

120g stiff wheat starter with 50% hydration
50ml whole milk
230ml water
40g wholegrain wheat flour
375g all purpose wheat flour (13% protein)
5g butter (or ghee) at room temperature
11g caster sugar
7g salt

Mix starter, milk and water in the bowl of a food processor. Then add flour and mix until well combined for a few minutes. Cover the bowl and let it rest for 45 minutes. Then add butter, sugar and salt and mix the dough at speed 2 until smooth for around 10 minutes. The final dough should be nice and smooth and not sticky.

Fold the dough like an envelope from the outside to the inside, transfer it to a lightly oiled container and cover with a lid. Let the dough rise for 3–4 hours at room temperature, and fold the dough twice again during this period.

Transfer the dough to a table sprinkled with flour, shape into a *boule* (round ball) and transfer it to a round proofing basket, sprinkled with starch or coarse flour. Leave for bulk fermentation for another 2 hours at room temperature – or ideally about 8–12 hours in the fridge.

Preheat the oven to 250°C (gas mark 9). Transfer the dough to a baking sheet and make a razor cut at an angle of 45 degrees, resembling a smile. Bake with steam (you can put a shallow tray of water at the bottom of the oven) on a well-heated pizza stone or metal tray for 20 minutes at 250°C (gas mark 9) and for another 20 minutes at 210°C (gas mark 6 or 7) without steam.

Let the *palyanytsya* cool down on a wire rack.

SYRNIKI

These small curd cheese pancakes are my favourite Ukrainian food, and I try to order them everywhere I go. Mostly for breakfast, sometimes for lunch, even for dessert. I miss them so much I tried many times to recreate them at home, and after advice from a host of Ukrainian friends, we ended up with this.

220g curd cheese (best to use full fat Polish *tvorog*, available in East European shops and big supermarkets)
40g cream cheese
1 egg yolk
½ tsp vanilla extract or paste
1 tbsp caster sugar
2 tbsp plain flour, plus extra to dredge
75g raisins (optional)
30ml sunflower oil

To serve
fresh berries or coulis
sour cream

Put the cheeses, egg yolk, vanilla, sugar plus two tablespoons of flour into a large bowl and blend together with a stick blender (or you can just use a fork) until relatively smooth.

Stir through the raisins, if using.

Cover and leave in the fridge for at least 30 minutes, or overnight. This will help the flour absorb some moisture from the cheese and make them easier to shape.

Divide into small balls – about 20 to 25 grams each – and flatten with the palm of your hand. Dredge in flour on both sides.

Fry the *syrniki* in sunflower oil on a medium-low heat for about 3 minutes each side, until a gentle golden brown and cooked through in the middle.

Serve with fresh berries or coulis, and sour cream.

GOMBOVTSI

This is a traditional Ukrainian dish originating from Zakarpattia, prepared with full fat curd cheese with various fruit fillings. *Gombovtsi* are usually steamed and covered in fried breadcrumbs with added sugar.

Mykhailo Lazarev of Snidanishna says: 'We prepare *gombovtsi* with cherry filling and serve them with strained home-made *ryazhenka*, or baked milk. We've slightly adapted this dish for our restaurant and instead of steaming the dumplings, we boil them in water. The recipe is very simple and easy to prepare!'

400g full fat curd cheese or Polish *tvorog*
100g semolina
50g caster sugar, plus extra for the fried breadcrumbs
7g vanilla sugar or ½ tsp real vanilla paste
2 egg whites
60g cherries (fresh or frozen) without stones
60g plain flour
50g butter
100g breadcrumbs, fried in 10g butter until golden, crisp and dry

To serve
500ml home-made *ryazhenka*, baked milk, which you can sometimes find in Polish shops or online, or thick yoghurt, with honey or caramel
cherry compote or jam
hazelnuts, toasted

If using *ryazhenka*: a day before preparing the *gombovtsi*, pour the *ryazhenka* onto a double-folded cheesecloth and hang it over a container overnight in the fridge. This will drain any excess whey and make the *ryazhenka* into a thick sour-cream like consistency.

The next day, press the curd cheese through a fine sieve or blend with a stick blender to make it smooth.

Add semolina, sugar and vanilla sugar or vanilla paste, mix well with a spoon, then add the two egg whites and mix again.

Cover the mixture and leave in the fridge for 40 minutes so that the semolina absorbs some of the moisture from the cheese.

Divide the mixture into small balls – around 18 to 20 grams each.

Place the cherries on a napkin and dry them a little to make them easier to work with.

Sprinkle flour on the table, flatten each cheese ball out, then place a cherry in the centre and wrap it carefully inside, making sure that it is perfectly sealed – then roll the ball on a little flour.

Bring a large saucepan of water to the boil. When all the balls are stuffed with cherries, cook them in the boiling water for 3–4 minutes. You may need to do this in several batches so as not to overcrowd the pan.

Melt the butter in another pan and as soon as the *gombovtsi* bob to the surface, take them out carefully with a slotted spoon and put them into the butter, swirling them around gently so all sides are covered.

Mix the fried breadcrumbs with sugar to taste, then roll the buttered *gombovtsi* in the sweetened crumbs.

On a warm plate, spread the thick strained *ryazhenka*. Alternatively, spread thick yoghurt sweetened with honey or caramel. Place the finished *gombovtsi* on top, with some cherry compote or jam and toasted hazelnuts.

Mykhailo says: 'This dish is not very sweet, so at the restaurant we serve our *gombovtsi* with cherry compote and toasted hazelnuts. They are ideal with some Carpathian herbal tea for breakfast or as a dessert after the main course. If it all seems a bit too complicated, you can always find this dish on the menu at our Snidanishna restaurant in Kharkiv.'

BANOSH

This is from Valerii, the chef with the call sign Maestro, from the Bud De, Druzhe group. They make a dehydrated version which is sealed into a long-life pack for soldiers serving at the front line to reconstitute with hot water. Here is the fresh version to make from scratch.

750ml full fat milk
250ml sour cream
100g cornmeal or fine polenta
½ tsp salt

For the topping
1 small onion, thinly sliced
30–50ml sunflower oil
300g mushrooms, sliced
1 handful of fresh dill, chopped
75g feta cheese, crumbled

In a large saucepan, bring the milk and sour cream to a gentle boil over a low heat.

Keeping the heat on low, gradually add the cornmeal, stirring constantly with a balloon whisk so that it doesn't burn.

Add the salt and continue to cook, stirring all the time, until it thickens and begins to come away from the side of the pan, this should take about 5–10 minutes.

For the topping, fry the onion in sunflower oil in a frying pan until soft and golden brown. Remove from the pan and fry the mushrooms until they start to brown, and throw the onions back in for a minute or two so that they cook together. Add a handful of dill, then serve it over the *banosh* with the crumbled feta cheese.

NIKA'S TRADITIONAL ODESA *FORSHMAK*

Nika says her mum makes outstanding *forshmak*. The recipe is extremely easy, as long as you can find the right kind of herring – lightly brined, not smoked, not too salted. Nika prefers it kept in brine, but the kind kept in oil is also fine. In the UK you can find similar herring in Polish shops – taste them first, and if they are already quite vinegary there is no need to add the extra vinegar in the recipe.

30ml wine vinegar (substitute part or all water if your herring already has some vinegar)
50g soft challah or other good-quality white bread, crusts cut off
200g herring fillets
1 granny smith apple, peeled, cored and cut into chunks
½ white onion, about 60g, cut into chunks
70g walnuts
50ml sunflower oil

To serve
dark rye bread
lacto-fermented cucumbers, tomatoes or apples

Sprinkle vinegar or water over bread, to soften it.

Put all the ingredients apart from the oil into a food processor. Pulse the mixture on a low speed and gradually add the oil, allowing the mixture to blend together, without turning it into a paste.

Some versions of the recipe cut the fish into small cubes by hand, or use a meat grinder.

Serve with the dark rye bread and lacto-fermented cucumbers, tomatoes or apples.

Nika says: 'There is a huge range of different kinds of *forshmak* in Odesa and in Ukraine. Some of them include hard boiled eggs. Some have cottage cheese. The dish became popular in our region during the times when Jewish people were only allowed to live within an area called the Pale of Settlement and could only work in certain low paid jobs, so families had to use whatever they had at home to make often oversalted and cheap herring taste good. If they were lucky enough to have chickens, they would add a hard boiled egg.'

NIKA'S MUSHROOM *YUSHKA* SOUP

This is a rich, deeply flavoured broth packed with vegetables – perfect on a cold winter day. It has three stages but nothing is too complicated.

For the dark mushroom broth
70g dried ceps (or other dried mushrooms)
3 litres hot water
300g onions
200g carrots
100g celery
100g trimmings from fresh mushrooms
80ml sunflower or other neutral oil
seasoning: bay leaf, thyme, black pepper whole, garlic, chilli, parsley, salt

For the zazharka
200g carrots
220g celeriac
150g onions
1 clove of garlic
30ml sunflower oil
salt

For the fried mushrooms
500g of any seasonal fresh mushrooms (off season you can use regular chestnut or button mushrooms)
50ml sunflower oil
50g butter
salt

To serve
sour cream
fresh parsley
spring onions

Cover the dried mushrooms with 1.5 litres of hot water. Let it rehydrate so all of the flavours incorporate into the liquid. Set aside for about 30 minutes while preparing the rest of the ingredients.

Peel and roughly chop all the vegetables. Start by heating the oil in a heavy-bottom pan, then add the vegetables for the broth and cook on a medium heat. Finely chop the garlic and add when the vegetables have softened, then cook until everything has taken on a light golden colour.

Drain the soaked mushrooms (keep the precious liquid to use next) and add to the pan as well.

Next, add the liquid from soaking the mushrooms, another 1.5 litres of hot water and all the seasoning.

Bring to a boil, turn down the heat and let it simmer for 40 minutes. Strain your beautiful bouillon broth so it's nice and clear.

For the *zazharka*, cut the carrots, celeriac and onions into fine dice – known as *brunoise* – and cook gently in a frying pan with sunflower oil. Finely chop the garlic and add when the vegetables have softened. Cook until everything has taken on a light golden colour. Season with salt. Set aside.

Cut the fresh mushrooms into evenly sized two-centimetre pieces. In the same frying pan, fry until golden in sunflower oil and butter, adding salt to taste. Set aside.

Cook together the dark mushroom broth, fried mushrooms and *zazharka* for about ten minutes, so that the flavours mix together well, and taste to check if the soup is seasoned enough.

Serve with sour cream, chopped fresh parsley and spring onions.

You can also make it with boiled potatoes and/or barley, if you want your mushroom *yushka* to be more hearty.

KATRYA'S POPPYSEED CAKE WITH PLUMS

Every time I visit Katrya in Lviv, there is always a piece of cake to try. This one, with sticky caramelised plums and poppyseeds, is especially delicious. It uses six egg whites and Katrya suggests making custard with the leftover yolks, should you have the time and inclination. It is equally good with thick yoghurt or cream.

20g brown sugar
1/2 tsp cinnamon
500g plums, de-stoned
6 egg whites
lemon juice
140g caster sugar
160g plain flour
1 tsp baking powder
50g poppy seeds
110g butter, melted
icing sugar (optional)

Preheat the oven to 175°C/160°C fan/gas mark 3. Prepare a 25 x 25 cm baking tin by greasing lightly and lining it with baking parchment. Sprinkle the base with a mixture of brown sugar and cinnamon.

Cut the de-stoned plums into quarters and lay them tightly on the sugared base of the tin.

Place the egg whites in a clean bowl, add a few drops of lemon juice and beat them with an electric whisk until stiff peaks form.

Turn the bowl over – if the whites stay put it means they are whisked enough.

Add the caster sugar in stages and continue to beat.

Add the flour, baking powder and poppy seeds and gently fold through the mixture with a spoon until smooth.

Now add melted butter (it should be barely warm, not hot!) and mix gently but thoroughly until smooth.

Spoon the cake mixture on top of the plums in an even layer.

Bake on the middle shelf of the oven for 45–50 minutes, and then remove the cake and let it cool on a rack.

Turn the cake out onto a plate so the plums are on top. Carefully peel away the baking parchment, and, if you like, sprinkle the cake with icing sugar.

ENERGY BARS INSPIRED BY
DOU BAKERY, ODESA

The bakers at DOU make huge trays of these nutritious and delicious bars to send to their military friends on the front line. They will keep in an airtight container in the fridge for several days.

200g prunes
200g raisins
2 medium eggs
200g caster sugar
180g plain flour
40g rye flour
1½ tsp baking powder
1 tsp salt
200g smooth peanut butter
50g soft butter
75g salted peanuts
½ tsp cardamom
½ tsp cinnamon
½ tsp vanilla extract

Preheat the oven to 175°C/160°C fan/gas mark 3. Line an 8 x 12 cm metal baking tin with baking parchment.

Soak the prunes and raisins in boiling water for 10 minutes and then drain, discarding the liquid. Blend with a stick blender into a rough paste.

With the whisk attachment in a stand mixer, whisk the eggs and caster sugar until light and frothy.

Switch to the beater attachment. Mix in the flours, baking powder and salt, then add the prune and raisin mixture, the peanut butter and the butter, the peanuts, spices and vanilla. Mix thoroughly, scraping down to make sure everything is fully incorporated. It will be a very thick mixture.

Spoon it into the prepared tray and smooth the top, then bake for 18–20 minutes.

Leave to cool before cutting into bars.

ACKNOWLEDGEMENTS

I would like to thank everyone who took part in this book, the volunteers who trusted and befriended me enough to let me travel huge distances with them to difficult places, and the chefs, cooks and businesses who let me spend time with them too... I am very fortunate to have met you and to have learned so much in the process.

I must start with thanks to our Bake for Ukraine team in Odesa – Maria Kalenska, Lena, Olha, Oleg, and Oleksandr Baron, who also took photos for this book – you are all the absolute best of humanity and the bright future of Ukraine. And to our volunteers abroad – Mykola, Olga, Alexandre, Andrew and the many wonderful supporters who have raised funds and helped us with essential logistics. And Yura: thank you for your service.

Many of the people I interviewed for this book spoke to me in English, for which I am profoundly grateful. But I also worked with some fantastic fixers and translators, including Odesa journalist Artem and Yevhen in Kharkiv, who were so professional and eternally helpful – huge thanks to both of you.

Thanks also to Svitlana in London and Kharkiv, Marcin in Kharkiv region, Maya and Yevhen in Dnipro, Andrii in Saltivka – I am so grateful for all your interpreting and logistic skills, and for your friendship.

Special thanks to Maria and Andrii in Kyiv who have not only been the most generous hosts but also managed to make my vaguest and most random requests happen, on a regular basis. Maria, thank you for showing me Kharkiv and helping me navigate everything from blackouts to travel arrangements – it continues to be an education.

None of this would have happened, of course, without my agent and publisher who believed in this book and gave me the confidence to go ahead.

Thank you so much to Heather Holden-Brown for taking me on in the first place – and the determination to keep pushing and find the right home for my stories. And to the wonderful Elly James for taking it all the way after Heather's retirement.

To Hannah MacDonald at September Publishing – I can't thank you enough for having faith in me, and for all your professionalism and patience which has guided me through the whole experience. Huge thanks also to Charlotte Cole for overseeing and piloting the final process – and to Seán Costello for the excellent copy editing.

I want to thank the whole team at Duckworth and Read Maxwell – Matt, Olivia, Claire and Rob. It's a real pleasure to work with you all.

I'm very grateful to my employers at ITN and Channel 4 News for being so supportive and for allowing me to take a sabbatical to spend time in Ukraine.

Thank you to everyone who read early drafts of chapters, especially Kate who provided really helpful notes and guidance, and Natasha who generously gave me the benefit of her book publishing experience. And Olia Hercules, you are constantly an inspiration.

To my many friends in Ukraine, who have become like a second family: special mention to Dmytro from Antytila for his energy and courage, to Lila, Olia, Valeriia and Viktoria – the Odesa sisters, Oleg V and the many volunteers who do such extraordinary things without hesitation.

And of course I have to thank all the incredible chefs, bakers and cooks who contributed recipes, and whose food I have enjoyed in the most difficult and challenging circumstances you could imagine. There are too many for me to mention everyone here, but thanks must go in Odesa to Illia and Viacheslav at DOU, Nika and her team at Dizyngoff, Nazar, Aleksander, Vika, Kostya and all the amazing home cooks in the city and around Bessarabia who Maria introduced me to. In Kyiv, to Igor Mezencev who gave me the best insights into Ukrainian food, Stanislav Zavertailo, Vlad and Yulia, Vova Tashaev and the team from Bakehouse. In Kharkiv – Tetiana at Pouhque, Dima and the team at Makers, everyone at Snidanishna and Mykyta at Tripichya. I now have a *syrniki* habit for life.

I am writing this in a Kyiv kitchen lit by torchlight during yet another blackout: I hope so much that Ukrainians will have the peaceful life again which they deserve. In the meantime, I would like to pay tribute to the courage, the resilience and the generosity which I witness here every day.

For more information about Vova and Lyuda Korniicha, see https://www.theguardian.com/world/2023/oct/03/windows -ukraine-donations-help-villagers-rebuild-shattered-homes.

HOW TO DONATE

If you'd like to donate directly to the groups working on the ground in Ukraine:

To help fund the future of **Bake for Ukraine's** mobile bakeries, and the bakeries that make free bread and distribute it to communities in need: bakeforukraine.org

To support inclusive bakery **Good Bread for Good People** in Kyiv, who also bake and distribute free bread: goodbread.com.ua

The British registered charity – the **Legacy of War Foundation** – does incredible work in Ukraine and other conflict zones around the world, giving targeted support directly to communities by partnering with local, grassroots organisations: legacyofwarfoundation.com

ABOUT THE AUTHOR

Felicity Spector has been a television journalist for thirty-five years, starting her career covering the fall of the Communist bloc and the end of the old Soviet Union. She worked as Moscow producer for ITN between 1990–92 and visited Ukraine when it declared independence. An influential Instagrammer and Substacker, she has built a following of more than 110,000 with a fascinating account that depicts her after-work adventures in restaurants and home baking. She has been spending all her spare time volunteering in Ukraine since summer 2022, helping to support the work of Bake for Ukraine. @felicityspector